Commercial Crises of the Nineteenth Century by H.M. Hyndman
First Prism Key Press Edition 2012

Prism Key Press
New York, NY 10001
PrismKeyPress.com

ISBN-13: 978-1475029253

Commercial Crises of the Nineteenth Century

H.M. Hyndman

CONTENTS

Preface

It suggested itself to me to write this little book when I read certain letters which appeared in the **Times** last year in answer to some letters of my own in that journal on *The Coming Crisis in Trade*. My opponents, it was manifest, had never carefully considered how it came about that these crises should continually recur during a period when the power of mankind to produce wealth was increasing with After rapidity than ever before in the history of world. I have endeavoured in the following s to give a brief but, I hope, clear sketch of such crises during the present century.

My indebtedness to Herr Max Wirth's elaborate work, **Geschichte der Handelskrisen**, in regard to the details of the earlier crises, I hereby cordially acknowledge.

H.M.H.
LONDON, *February,* 1892

Introduction

The causes and effects of industrial crises must be reckoned among the most important subjects for consideration in the concluding years of the nineteenth century. From time to time all civilised countries are now exposed to a complete upset of their industrial, commercial, and financial machinery, at the very moment when the great majority even of those who are directly engaged in business imagine that trade is at its best and that no danger threatens them. Suddenly, in the midst of the greatest apparent prosperity, when the promoters and contractors have their hands full of work; when merchants and traders are congratulating themselves on the extent of their turnover; when manufacturers, mine-owners and shipping companies are dividing most satisfactory profits; and when the workers are being paid a somewhat better rate of wages – at that juncture a change for the worse begins. Prices, which have risen all along the line of commodities that enter into our social life, fall with great rapidity, uneasiness and distrust spread throughout the business community, there is a rush to obtain money either by sales of securities and goods, or by obtaining advances from the banks; and a nation, or as is now commonly the case, a whole group of nations, finds itself in the midst of a dangerous crisis, without knowing the why or the wherefore of the crash.

Now if this recurrence of financial and industrial disasters could be traced to well-defined natural causes, mankind would, in this as in other cases, be compelled to accept the inevitable, and make preparations to lessen the mischief which may be done. Earthquakes, droughts, tidal waves, hurricanes, swarms of locusts, epidemics, have all brought about serious disturbances in trade at different times; and some of the disturbances thus occasioned have had more than local or temporary effects. As science advances and knowledge spreads, we may succeed in counteracting some of the injury done to society by these convulsions of nature, and in limiting the ravages due to others which are in a certain degree open to human control. But nobody imagines that they will ever be finally stopped, or that within a conceivable period our descendants will have the power to order the winds and waves to be still, even if drought proves to be, like monarchs, amenable to skilfully-used explosives in the higher air.

Many of the trade difficulties of ancient times and of the middle ages can be directly traced to drought, or to flood, in the same way that famine due to similar causes has a prejudicial effect upon commerce in China, in India, in Russia, and even to a certain extent in Europe and America to-day. Such troubles, it is universally recognised now-a-days, should be met by freely using the surplus of one country, or one district, to make up the deficiency in another. Formerly, periods of scarcity were prepared for by the establishment of granaries and grain pits, which were not opened until such time as the failure of the crops in the particular region affected had deprived the people of their annual food supply; and it is more than probable that, our modern zeal for applying the latest methods of western civilisation to communities quite a different stage of social and economical development, this method for providing against a rainless day has been foolishly abandoned.

It is certain, at any rate, that at no period prior to the growth of what is now known as the capitalist system of production – the system of production, that is to say, of articles of social for profit, by free labourers who are paid wages – did difficulties arise in the trade or finance of any community from an actual superfluity of the wealth which the members of that community needed in their daily life. Famine, in former generations, of course attacked the poorer members of society first, and in the ancient slave-supported civilisations, as well as under the feudal regime, the contrast between the well-being of the few in "hard times," as compared with the want and misery of the many, was in some respects as striking as it is today. But still the crucial distinction between our own and any former period in the world's history remains – that the times of greatest distress for the mass of the people now are the times when there is a complete glut of the commodities which they need and which they make.

Local gluts and national crises due to the same cause, which now take so wide a range, have been recorded before the present century. Economists were anxious to account for them, and philanthropists were eager to remedy them, in the seventeenth and eighteenth centuries. As the growing influence of the middle-classes due to the extension of their political power was felt, and as the restrictions imposed by the elaborate balancing of interests in the feudal system slowly gave way before the spread of commerce and the widening of the local into a national market, the tendency to inflation followed by corresponding depression made itself manifest more clearly.

The local difficulty of transmitting goods produced for profit into money appeared then as a national difficulty. At the end of the seventeenth century such crises were recognised and partially analysed by John Bellers, who, in a passage quoted by me some years ago from his **College of Industry**, puts the matter thus: "In the common way of living on trade, men, their wives or children, often lose half what they get either by dear bargains, bad debts or law suits of which there will be neither in the college; and if the earth gives but forth its fruit, and workmen do but their parts, they will have plenty; whereas now, the husbandmen and mechanics both are ruined, though the first have a great crop and the second industriously maketh much manufacture. Money and not labour being made the standard, the husbandman paying the same rent and wages as when the crop yielded double the price; it being no better with the mechanics, where it's not who wants his commodity, but who can give him money for it (will keep him), and so often he must take half the value in money another would give him in labour that hath no money."

Here the difficulty is to bring the two producers of wealth together by reason of the necessity for converting commodities into money. Though also in this case a particular set of workers are spoken of as if they were producing for their own profit, the fact, of course, is that, under the system of production in which the capitalist class employs the wage-earners to reduce, the profit is realised by the employers and not by the actual producers.

Now, so long as the labourer, be he husband-man or mechanic, makes goods for his own use, or to the direct order of his customers, or for the supply of a local and limited market, he is in control of his tools, of his farm or workshop, of his raw material, and owns his product. Thus, though he does produce primarily for his own individual advantage, and not, as was the case under the old communal and gentile arrangements, for the advantage of the whole society in which he himself was included as a unit, yet he is not producing wholly and solely with a view to exchange on a great general market; and, above all, his products are owned by him, and are dealt with under his own control. So soon, however, as in the course of economical development, the workers began to produce no longer as individuals for their own use, or for the direct use of others in their locality, but as wage-earners, bound together by no tie other than that of turning out commodities or articles of use in the social conditions of the time to the order of an employer who threw the goods on the market; so soon as they did this a direct antagonism was established between the two parts of the wealth-creating machine.

The workers were then working no longer as individuals; they were working together in social union, and, as

12

division of labour came in, were working together in co-operative union for a social purpose – namely, to produce goods which were articles of no use to them for the use of others at a distance, the limits of whose wants they could not gauge, although these were supplied by the exercise of a social function, to wit, exchange. In these circumstances the actual producers of the goods have no control over the raw material, no ownership of the finished article, no say in the matter of exchange, and, in the complete form of the process as we see it to-day, no proprietorship in the tools or machinery. They are simply wage-earners, working at wages regulated by the average standard of life or subsistence in their trade; which wages represent only a fraction of the value of the commodities produced by their labour. But the capitalist or employer, he has still retained the right of individual appropriation or ownership, and with it the power to exchange, which formerly belonged to the individual workers. The workers are working socially for social objects: the employer appropriates individually, and exchanges for individual objects – the realisation of his profits namely. Thus we have here a distinct and definite antagonism lying at the very basis of our modern system of wealth-creation, an antagonism between the social form of the actual production and the individual form of the appropriation and exchange.

Now, the remarkable point about the position of thought in regard to political economy to-day is that the orthodox political economists, and even some who call themselves socialists, fail to discern this antagonism even when it is pointed out to them. Not a few still maintain, also, that there is no antagonism between the labourers and the capitalists; in this respect proving themselves less clear-sighted than their master, Adam Smith, who, at least, detected that employers were in a permanent conspiracy to keep down the rate of wages.

But it is precisely this original antagonism between social production for social purposes and individual

13

appropriation and exchange for individual profit that gives the key to all the industrial, commercial, and financial difficulties which arise in our society at the present time.

Failing this key, the most absurd explanations are given of those modern crises arising from superfluity and glut, followed by the discharge of work-people and the general distress, which occasion such grave anxiety to every thinking man.

Thus the problem of crises has been confidently solved by a reference to over-population, and there are still not a few wiseacres left who persist in this explanation; though it has been conclusively proved time after time that the power of man to produce wealth is increasing in every civilised country in a far more rapid ratio than any increase of population ever recorded among the poorest nations in the world. Though, moreover, it is seen at each successive crisis that a country which, like the United States in 1856 and 1872, had no over-population, and could have no over-population, before the crisis, had hundreds of thousands, not to say millions of people, out of work or employed at half-time when the crisis came. Manifestly, therefore, the over-population theory in nowise touches even the fringe of the problem.

Then there are those who enlarge upon the dangers of over-production, and consider that here we have the undoubted cause of crises. But this is to restate the problem, not to solve it, seeing that at the time when this "overproduction," thanks to the enormous power of modern machinery, has been pushed to its last point, there are thousands of people who stand in need of the results of the over-production, and would gladly give their labour and its product in return for some of these very articles, including not unfrequently food itself, which have been so overproduced.

There are, again, the currency quacks who attribute everything to the lack of sufficient means of circulating

14

commodities; though the same phenomena precisely have been recorded when currency was somewhat restricted, as, prior to the gold-discoveries in America and Australia, gold coin certainly was; and when it is if anything too plentiful, as during the crisis of 1857 it may be taken to have been. Similarly, it has been suggested that the system of banking is to blame, though here again it is impossible to show how tinkering with credit based upon production can remedy the defects of the faulty system of production itself.

To such a pitch of despair have economists been driven in their anxiety to avoid the true solution propounded for them already by a greater thinker than themselves, that Mr. Stanley Jevons traced crises to periods of bad harvests, and then, triumphantly connecting bad harvests with spots on the sun, referred the whole of our social troubles in this particular to these strange changes in that great body. This theory was actually accepted for a time, until what was perhaps the worst crisis of the century came in the same year with one of the finest harvests ever known on the planet, and when also the sun's disc was exceptionally afflicted with spots. Then it became apparent to the most credulous that the spots on the sun had as much influence on industrial crises as the spots on the leopard in the Zoological Gardens; and that the genius before whose shrine our Professors of Political Economy at Oxford and Cambridge still prostrate themselves had only added another to his long list of blunders.

The ablest summary of the causes of crises yet formulated outside of the school of Marx is really but a recapitulation of the symptoms which precede a crisis, not in any sense an analysis of the causes which bring it about. A rush into new enterprises and a mania for speculation; an eager anxiety to get rich without toil; the credulity of the public in accepting unsound enterprises; the increase of luxury; the rise of prices; the exceptional demand for labour and increase of wages, etc., etc. – all these are precursors of an industrial crisis, but they cannot be considered as more than effects of what is going on below all the time.

To return, therefore, to the view already set forth. We have historically on record the origin of the antagonism between that social form of production and individual form of appropriation of commodities which replaced the limited individual production of the middle ages. Thus, the workers, though nominally free, lost all control over the products of their labour, and could in no wise direct or influence either the nature or the disposal of the commodities. From this time forward all improvements in machinery, and all the conquests of science as applied to the increase of wealth, have come into the hands of the employing class, who, by degrees, relieved themselves of all trade regulations and State or municipal restrictions, and went forward to capture and control new markets for their goods. With the industrial revolution at the end of the eighteenth century and the establishment of the factory system, this monopoly of improvements in the hands of the employing class became more and more dangerous to the welfare of the community.

For now the antagonism to which reference has been made began to show itself on a wider scale than was possible before. Each manufacturer is, of course, solely anxious to make hay while the sun shines. When, therefore, markets are good, he produces as much of the special commodities he manufactures as he possibly can, he employs more "hands," or works those he has overtime in order to gain greater and greater profits while prices are high. All do the same thing at the same time, no one having the slightest regard in the heat of competition for the interests of his neighbour manufacturer or for the glut of the market which may ensue. This arises from the inherent nature of the competitive system in its first hey-day of youth and prosperity. Every employer and capitalist, in order to live himself, must try his hardest to extend and not merely to maintain his trade. Good employers and bad employers there may be, but no capitalist, so long as competition is the rule in his trade, can help proceeding in this way. The moment he relaxes his efforts, down he goes in the struggle, his firm appears in the bankruptcy court, and the fury of competition rages on as before over his business remains.

But this cannot go on permanently. Though the markets are larger than ever they were, and the cheapening of goods perpetually going on enables the machine industry to conquer the old forms of production in other countries, nevertheless, the crisis is approaching. There is no social control whatever exercised over the individual rush for profit. As the labour in the factory, in the works, in the mine, on the farm is more and more completely organised and ordered, so do the anarchy and disorder more and more completely dominate in the exchange. While inside all is conducted with the most careful regard to the profit-making efficiency of all the parts, outside each contends against his fellow to sell his goods most rapidly and in the greatest quantity.

Moreover, the necessities of the capitalist system force the manufacturer, or contractor, or mine-owner, or shipbuilder, continuously to realise his value embodied in goods, or railways, or coal, or iron, or vessels, in the shape of cash. Without doing this he cannot recommence his operations by buying raw material, fuel, oil, labour-force and the like. The commodities produced by other manufactures are of no use to him, any more than his commodities are of use to them. Each and all must realise their products in coin or its equivalent. However good a firm's credit may be, to this complexion must they all come at last. Consequently, the capitalist system of production involves an antagonism between money and commodities.

If the circulation of the capitalist's commodities is

checked, or the realisation of his paper representing work done is impeded, then the work cannot be carried on at all, but must be stopped altogether. But before this point is reached, doubts arise as to whether matters have not been pushed too far. There is a rush to discount bills and to obtain advances on securities, or to sell out and out for cash at reduced prices. But just as everybody before was anxious to produce more on the rising prices, and buyers were eager to buy – not for use but for profit – so all now are looking about to see how they can contrive to produce less, and those who were buyers are eager to sell, no longer to obtain enhanced profits, but to avoid actual loss. A crisis has, in fact, set in, and what should be the gain of society becomes its direct injury. That increased power to create wealth on which men are in the habit of congratulating themselves, becomes an actual hindrance to the creation of more wealth. That is to say, the sole object of capitalists in producing commodities is to obtain profits for themselves. Their individual control and anarchical method has resulted in a glut. That glut renders it impossible for them to continue to produce on the same scale. Therefore, many of them go into bankruptcy, and many more close their factories and works, or run them on short time. Hence labourers thrown out of work, goods unsaleable, and at intervals a commercial and financial crash.

What has happened? The capitalist class has virtually declared its own inability to conduct the business of the community. The form of the production has revolted against the form of the exchange.

As a result, prices fall all along the line, economies are resorted to, mostly at the expense of the workers: and in due course, after a period more or less prolonged of stagnation and depression, the heavy accumulations of stocks are disposed of, confidence is gradually restored, orders begin to come in afresh, and the whole cycle is repeated, ending in a similar crisis on probably a larger scale than before. Such crises with the liquidations that follow upon them now frequently extend over many years. The power of production hampers its continuous employment. So far as the actual producers are concerned, the destruction of the goods manufactured would be a direct benefit. They have been employed in producing their worst enemy and bringing about their own discharge. Men, that is, in civilised communities, are now controlled and overmastered by their own machinery of production, instead of controlling and mastering it themselves for the general advantage.

To formulate the diagnosis of the evil is, in fact, to point out the only possible remedy. This remedy society itself is unconsciously beginning to supply. In every direction the unregulated capitalist competitive system is being modified and partially transformed. How the changes which are now being brought about, unconsciously and anarchically, may in the near turn be carried on consciously and in an orderly fashion by an educated and organised democracy, will be partially suggested in the concluding chapter of this work. Meanwhile recognition of the economic and class antagonisms in which our civilised society moves and has its being is slowly making way even among so whose position is threatened by the coming change.

I. The Crisis of 1815

The first important crisis of the nineteenth century occurred under quite exceptional circumstances, and though not entirely confined to Great Britain, this country was chiefly affected by it. This crisis of 1815 came immediately upon the conclusion of the peace on the downfall of Napoleon. It was generally believed that immediately after the signature of the treaty of peace at Paris a period of great commercial prosperity would begin, and that England in particular would reap the fruits of her supremacy at sea and of the great development of her internal resources which had taken place during the war. Such exertions had never before been made, nor such expenditure incurred, by any nation.

The weight of taxation was crushing during the war, the drain for men and material was unprecedented on so small a population, and so great was the stringency in the precious metals that the Bank of England had suspended specie payments since 1797. In 1756 the funded debt of the United Kingdom was little more than £72,000,000, in 1815 it was £800,000,000. The public expenditure in 1814 was no less than £106,832,260, in 1815 it was £92,000,000, and two years later only £55,000,000. Tens of thousands of men were then set free from the useless services of war to devote themselves to increasing the wealth of the country; the markets of the Continent, long nominally, at least, closed to English goods, were thrown open; and a fine harvest at home helped on, as it was thought, the general improvement due to the beneficial change in foreign affairs.

Precisely the contrary, however, of that which was expected took place. Great Britain had been enabled to hold her own during the long war of twenty-two years, had subsidised half Europe against the French, and had supported a weight of taxation previously unknown, because during these twenty-two years the great machine industry and the extension of commerce poured into the pockets of her trading and land-owning classes untold wealth. Napoleon's policy of excluding English goods from Europe had forced our manufacturers and merchants to seek outlets for their cotton, iron, wool, and other manufactures farther afield. They found their new markets, thanks to the complete supremacy of England at sea, in India, North and South America, the West India Islands, and Asia Minor, pushing their trade over, the whole known world with the greatest vigour. The cheapness of English goods became the marvel of the universe, and the machine-made stuffs of Lancashire and Yorkshire gave an impulse to English commerce scarcely equalled even during the period of railway construction and the gold discoveries. Hargreaves and Jennings, and Arkwright and Watt, the first fruits of machinery, and the early application of steam, piled up riches for England; and military and naval victories were made possible by extraordinary commercial success.

But now there was peace. The great European markets close at hand were again open to our trade, and every preparation was made to take full advantage of this great opportunity. Scarcely a manufacturer in business had failed to take time by the forelock and produce more than his usual quantity of goods, with a view to disposing of them on the Continent. The truth was, however, that English commodities had never been so completely shut out as supposed. Cheapness had broken down the Custom-House barriers, and smuggling, winked at by officials, had developed the proportions of a regular trade. In addition, Continental manufacturers, though lagging behind their English competitors in some branches of business, had not been wholly neglectful of the changes in the form of production. They, too, were beginning to produce the new machinery, and with the aid of steam.

Thus, in all districts which English goods were obliged to reach by long land transport, the native manufacturers had the advantage. No account of these facts was taken at the time, and it was hastily assumed that if, under all the drawbacks of smuggling and possible confiscation, twelve millions sterling worth of English goods could be profitably delivered at foreign ports, certainly not less than double that quantity might safely be disposed of now that peace had been firmly established. All rushed in at once to benefit by this exceptional opportunity. The result was that the foreign markets were speedily glutted. English goods were to be had cheaper at foreign ports than they could be bought for at their place of manufacture. For the foreign buyers had nothing to offer in exchange for these manufactures except their agricultural products. But these were shut out from the English markets by high duties. Corn, wine, and spirits could not be taken by English merchants owing to the tariffs, and as there was nothing else to offer, piles of English commodities lay unsaleable on the Continent, and either brought their owners nothing at all, or were "slaughtered" at ridiculous prices. Not only were numberless speculators ruined, but the manufacturers sustained terrible losses.

The good harvest itself did but seem to make matters worse. Everybody had become accustomed to high prices during the war. The land-owners and farmers had done well during the troubled period. Paper money at a discount of about twenty-five per cent., as compared with gold, was the general currency, and inflated prices ruled to an abnormal extent. All calculations for sale of agricultural produce had been based on the continuance of a similar state of things. But suddenly the change came, and with it so plentiful a harvest that the barns and storehouses were filled to repletion with grain, in the same way that the warehouses were choked with manufactured goods. There was a conspiracy of superfluity to impoverish all classes. Nobody knew what to do. The state of things transcended all experience. Crises and stagnation of trade had been known

23

before, but never on so large a scale. For in this case, as in those cases which follow, the cause of all the collapse of trade and general poverty was manifestly a superabundance of wealth.

The working people, who suffered most from the crisis, were little inclined to bear their misery silently. Discharged soldiers and sailors came in to compete on an already overstocked labour-market, and the attitude of the unemployed and starving labourers became threatening in the extreme. Observing that machinery was everywhere supplanting hand-labour, they not unnaturally jumped to the conclusion that these increased powers of producing wealth were really injurious to the workers, seeing that they were, in many instances, the direct cause of their want of employment. Bands of men consequently paraded the country smashing machinery, and demanding work and food.

The amount of machinery even then in use in Great Britain very far exceeded in power of production the total quantity of manual labour employed. But the war, that great and most extravagant customer to farmers, manufacturers, and other producers of wealth, having come to an end, those who were most anxious to obtain some of their superabundant supplies of food and manufactures in return for useful work were prevented from doing so by the fact that they could not be employed at a profit. Instead of increasing the number of their hands, and thus aggravating the glut, the one object of the producers was to lessen their output, until the accumulated stocks should be taken off the market, and they might, owing to rising prices, be able again to produce at a profit. If the stock in the farm buildings and warehouses had been burnt then, such was the irony of the situation, prosperity would have immediately recommenced on the same scale and for practically the same reasons as during the war.

At this very time, indeed, as during all such periods, the actual impoverishment, except for the working classes, was far more apparent than real. Even the Corn Laws, which were introduced in 1815 to keep up the price of grain, though the enactment occasioned a serious revolt in London, did not permanently check the growth of wealth; and, notwithstanding that exports fell from £51,000,000 in 1815 to £35,000,000 in 1817, the imports of cotton grew from 53,000,000 pounds in 1814 to 92,000,000 pounds in 1815, 86,000,000 pounds in 1816, and 116,000,000 pounds and 162,000,000 pounds in 1817 and 1818 respectively, while the population increased rapidly. The check, that is to say, on the growth of national wealth bore no proportion to the mischief inflicted on large portions of the population.

This crisis of 1815, though it had an effect upon the Continent and the various countries which traded to a considerable extent with the United Kingdom, could scarcely be called an international industrial crisis. In it, nevertheless, could be traced in the germ the peculiar phenomena of all the succeeding crises. Notably, we may observe the glut of commodities as the pre-eminent cause of lack of employment and misery for the working classes, already instanced by Robert Owen as directly due to the use of machinery by the great capitalists exclusively for their own profit. England, also, the victor in the great war, the country which had gained enormously in territory and influence during the struggle, underwent a far more trying crisis than France, the nation which had been completely overcome. In Great Britain the collapse of credit and the trade distress was very sharp, if short in its duration: in France there was practically no crisis at all. The very economical development which gave the English such resources to draw upon in war became a cause of commercial collapse on the conclusion of peace; in much the same way that Germany, after the victories of 1870, underwent a more serious shock than France, and the £200,000,000 of indemnity proved for the time, at any rate, rather a curse than a blessing to her people.

II. The Crisis of 1825

England, as a whole, speedily recovered from the industrial depression following upon the end of the great war. From the time when the Bank of England resumed specie payments completely in 1819, and indeed from the end of the year 1817, the upward movement of business became more and more rapid. A succession of good harvests helped on the revival of trade as the stocks of manufactured goods moved off; and the outcry of the agriculturists against the low price for grain was drowned by the din of the machinery in the cities working overtime, to great profit for the employers and constant employment for the "hands." The extension of trade seemed something phenomenal; the rapid accumulation of fortunes impelled the wealthy classes to undertake vast operations in every direction.

At the beginning of 1824, therefore, instead of grumbling and discontent, murmurs of satisfaction and gleeful anticipations of enhanced gains were heard from the capitalists on every side. By this time, too, even the agriculturists, who were producing larger and larger crops to the acre, began to share in the general prosperity. The average price of wheat for the year was 62s a quarter, yet no complaints were made, for the majority of the working population were in full employment. In the iron and coal industries, as well as in the cotton and wool factories, business was exceedingly brisk. Everybody was making haste to get rich. Speculation of the most reckless character far outstripped the limits of the most adventurous trading; and, so does history in a sense repeat itself, our growing relations with the South American States pushed this speculation to an almost unprecedented height. The mania affected the whole mercantile community, and extended to all the property-holding classes.

That such exceptional prosperity could not be altogether sound seems scarcely to have been suspected even by many of those who were capable of forming a clear judgment. The improved conditions of life for the middle-class were the theme of universal contentment. Such changes had been wrought in the appearance of town and country alike as are usually the result of several generations of continuous improvement. In the country, fields better tilled, barns and storehouses better built, horses, cattle, and sheep mere numerous and of better breeds. In the towns, an improved class of dwellings, greater comfort and luxury in every middle-class household. Division of labour pushed to a greater extent alike in production and distribution. An accumulation of money in the banks as well in London as in the provincial centres. A superabundance of capital seeking employment in the riskiest ventures. Projects of every kind for the construction of canals, tunnels, bridges, tramways, roads, and so forth, eagerly entertained and accepted. All proved that the savings of the middle-class, in spite of their increased expenditure on comfort, had more than kept pace with the growth of their wealth.

A complete change in the habits of this class was taking place. The unremitting and even excessive personal attention to the details of business was giving way to a more leisurely sort of existence for those who could now afford it. Instead of living in their houses of business, and working steadily day and night at their occupations, the well-to-do men of affairs and tradesmen of good standing began that plan of living in the suburbs, and going in during the day to their offices and shops, which has obtained so great an extension in our own times; while, at the same time, the lounger towns around our coasts began to attain considerable dimensions, owing to the visits and residence of Londoners.

In small matters, as in large, the change was very remarkable. The pinching and saving of the war times had given place to a more easy and generous view of life all round for the fairly well-to-do. It was a period of universal well-being for that class, accompanied, as statistics but too clearly show, by intense and grinding overwork for the masses of the people. Few thought of this at the time. All were content to congratulate the country on the singular prosperity and contentment, the wonderful sagacity and enterprise of that class of manufacturers and merchants, capitalists, bankers, shipowners, and tradesmen, who were regarded then, and for long afterwards, as the backbone of the nation. All was apparently based on the soundest foundations; everyone was convinced that this good fortune had been honestly earned, and would be solidly maintained. So hopeful was the tone of the period, so confident the anticipation of a bright future, that the most gloomy pessimist could scarcely see a dark cloud in the sky. Tomorrow shall be as to-day, and much more abundant, was chanted in chorus by hundreds or thousands of cool, calculating men, who, in the ordinary business of everyday life, we're shrewd and cautious enough.

The same nation which had gone through the great war against France with a determination and stolid persistence that astonished the world, which had stood up stoutly for its freedom at home, and had passed through the crisis already briefly sketched with comparatively trifling difficulty, now to all appearance lost its head entirely. All the best characteristics of the middle-class seemed to be swamped in one overmastering lust for gaming. The bubbles of the previous century were reblown in more glittering and fantastic shapes. The follies of 1824 and 1825 surpassed every previous financial folly. Classes of the population which had never before followed the-will-o'-the-wisps of speculation tumbled over one another in their eagerness to put salt on the tails of these flitlings of the financial marsh. It was highday and holiday for the Dousterswivels and John Laws, for unscrupulous schemers and half-insane enthusiasts. Everybody speculated in something: not only the world of business, but the entire population were swept along in the craze of gamblers. Old and young, men and women, rich and poor, noble and simple, one and all, were drawn into the throng. Even when all the purely absurd and swindling projects are eliminated, and only those are taken account of which have a reasonable claim to solidity, even then the scale of the commitments entered into by Great Britain are upon an astonishing scale – a scale rather suitable to the end than the beginning of the nineteenth century, and certainly more fitly representing the investments of twenty years than of two.

The amount of loans to foreign States, negociated in London or transferred to the London market during this period, in addition to a quantity of external loans, which were bought in England, but not being paid in London, were not quoted on the Stock Exchange, reached no less a total than £86,000,000.

Over and above these vast sums invested abroad, the following companies were established among others in 1824 and 1825:

	CAPITAL
20 Companies to build Railways,	£13,500,000
22 Bank and Insurance Companies,	£36,260,000
11 Gas Companies,	£8,000,000
17 Foreign Mining Companies,	£18,200,000
8 English and Irish Mining Companies,	£10,580,000
9 Companies for the construction of Canals, Docks, Steamers,	£10,580,000
27 Different Companies for various industrial businesses,	£12,000,000

The total amounting to 114 companies, with a gross capital of upwards of one hundred millions sterling. The shares of most of these companies stood at first at a high premium, and, in particular, the mining companies of Mexico and South America ran their shares up to a preposterous height; the Real del Monte with shares of a nominal value of £400, of which only £70 were paid up, were sold on the 2nd January, 1825, at £1,350 a share – that being two and a half times their quoted price only a month before.

The following passage might almost be read as referring not to 1824 but to 1889. "In the spring of 1824, when heavy payments had to be made on account of the South American loans and mining companies, so large an amount of gold and silver bullion was exported to South America that a sensible deficiency was caused in the available currency of Great Britain, and during the whole of the year 1824 and the first three months of 1825, the Bank of England materially increased its note circulation." At the same time the provincial banks, under a mischievous Act of Parliament passed in 1822, swamped the whole country with paper money, which found a ready outlet in that time of rising prices and universal speculation. In 1825 there were nearly thrice as many such notes out as there were in 1822, while between June, 1824, and October, 1825, from £10,000,000 to £12,000,000 of coined money was issued from the Mint. Every step was thus taken to encourage speculation to the point of actual danger to the State, and to inflate the existing inflation beyond all precedent.

So long as money could be obtained at a low rate of interest, and interest was maintained at a low rate by the enormous issue of small banknotes, the speculation went on; and, as has been said, all classes and both sexes took an active part in the scramble for wealth.

Few took into consideration the fact that the solid loans and enterprises undertaken called for more capital than the country had saved or could dispose of. The mania for fresh undertakings spread far and wide. In the single session of 1825, 438 applications were made for bills for private companies, and

286 charters were granted; in not a few cases causing grave suspicions to be aroused as to the uprightness of members of the House of Commons.

Canning had called in the New World to redress the balance of the Old, and English loan-mongers, merchants and promoters, as we have seen, put their own interpretation on the epigram. All considerations of geography, climate, native character, and disposition were thrown to the winds. Money was to be lent at good interest, merchandise was to be shipped to large profit, mines were to be opened to pay an unheard-of percentage in countries concerning which little or nothing was known to the majority of the speculators. The most ridiculous blunders were made by the class which was supposed to be carrying on business for the general benefit. Warming-pans were shipped to cities well within the tropics, and Sheffield carefully provided skaters with the means of enjoying their favourite exercise in regions where ice had never been seen. The best glass and porcelain were thoughtfully provided for naked savages, who had hitherto found horns and cocoa-nut shells quite hollow enough to hold all the drink they wanted.

One company was formed to provide the inhabitants of the River Plate with fresh butter, at a time when none but the wildest of wild cattle could be found from the Atlantic Ocean to the Andes; and a tribe of luckless Scotch dairymaids were shipped to Buenos Ayres, in order to milk cattle a trifle more savage than the Gaucho cowboys who herded. them. When the inconceivable difficulties of getting milk and cream in such circumstances had been at length overcome, and something in the shape of butter was provided, it was suddenly discovered that the misguided inhabitants preferred oil. Similar absurd blunders, sometimes with very tragic results alike for the unfortunate small investors as well as for the deluded emigrants, were of everyday occurrence. Such folly and madness would seem incredible did we not ourselves witness their recurrence in some form on each return of a period of prosperous trade. The wealth derived from the labours of the workers and the increased power of man over nature was played ducks and drakes with in every quarter of the globe, while at home, in England, this was perhaps the blackest time for the toilers and their children since the dark days of the sixteenth century.

Just when everything seemed most prosperous, the crisis – the first important international crisis of the capitalist epoch – was close at hand. Nine-tenths of the foreign ventures, it was soon apparent, would produce no return whatever, at any rate, for many years. Goods which had been thrown upon the market, as the inevitable result of working the new machinery at full power, and goods which had been kept off the market in the hope of prices being screwed up higher and higher yet, were suddenly found by their owners to be unsaleable at the prices even then ruling. Further advances were then sought from the bankers, who, the bank rate of discount being still low, at first stretched their resources to oblige their clients by discounting their paper at long dates. Then the calls upon the unpaid capital of the new issues began to come due, while no profits, of course, were as yet realised or likely to be realised. This led to further demands for accommodation. Men of business began to awaken from fancy to fact. The Bank of England, which had maintained its rate of discount low during the whole of the period of wild speculation, only raised it from 4 to 5 per cent. on the 17th December, 1825, when one great bank failure followed by others gave unmistakable warning of the coming crash.

And then the crash came. The very same people who had aggravated the over-speculation by their false and almost fraudulent finance, now rendered the collapse more disastrous by their panic-stricken precautions against the dangers they had themselves helped to evoke. In every direction the note issue was reduced, and credit was restricted to such an extent that even the bills of perfectly sound houses were rejected. Of course, in such circumstances the glut of unrealisable commodities on the market exceeded all limits. Prices fell all round with such alarming rapidity that even the most venturous buyers held aloof. Not only were speculators forced to relinquish their holdings, but the manufacturers, whose continual production necessitated realisations in cash, were compelled, failing further bank accommodation, to try to find the means of meeting their own bills by forced sales on the open market, or otherwise to close their mills and go into liquidation. The Stock Exchange could afford no relief; for shares which stood at an inconceivable premium yesterday were utterly valueless to-day. Everybody wanted to realise at once, and each was anxious to get out on the shoulders of his neighbour. Panic reigned supreme alike in finance and in business. The first great international crisis of the nineteenth century had begun.

In six weeks no fewer than seventy provincial banks failed. In London and in the country commercial houses fell one on the top of the other like a house of cards whose support is removed. Credit was almost at a standstill. It was impossible to say what constituted wealth for the purpose of carrying on business or meeting liabilities. The distrust was as profound as the confidence had but now been overweening. Whoever had loans out called them in; whoever had money in hand refused to part with it on any terms. From one end of Great Britain to the other people looked blankly in one another's faces, not knowing whence had arisen this sudden tornado of financial despair. Little else was discussed in the Exchange or on the market-place. While some said that the whole thing was purely imaginary, the result of foolish fears and scandalous rumours, others maintained with equal vigour that the crisis was but the beginning of the end, and that the downfall of our whole industrial and financial system was close at hand.

London endeavoured to check the panic by a great

meeting of wealthy merchants and bankers, who declared with the unanimity of the citizens of Ephesus that confidence would speedily be restored if people would only be confident. But the losers of the provinces refused to be comforted by the assurances of metropolitan magnates; and their practical reply to the blessed words of the greatest organisers of industry was a heavy run upon the great London banks. The anarchy of liquidation was as miserable a spectacle as the anarchy of speculation. The getting out was as disorderly and as disgusting as the getting in. Business got worse and worse, until the very productive power of the country was threatened with serious limitation by the uncertainty which weighed upon the entire community. Unless credit were in some way restored and the ordinary channels of trade accommodation were cleared, the winter of 1825 must prove unprecedentedly disastrous to the working population.

Whatever was done had to be done quickly. The Bank of England, whose directors were, as usual in trying times, at their wits' end, applied now to the Chancellor of the Exchequer to help them to remedy a state of things in part brought about by their own incompetence and want of foresight. The directors urged that unless they could give facilities for discount, which in existing circumstances they did not see their way to do, the crisis must continue, and ruin would overtake even the most sound and cautious establishments. Then, apparently for the first time in all this turmoil of excitement and hopeless confusion, the facts of the situation were faced. It was recognised that there was no reason why, because the greater part of the well-to-do classes and their hangers-on had hopelessly lost their heads, the ordinary business of the country should not again be placed on a sound basis. Excessive speculation and production, backed up by inflation of the currency and undue facilities for borrowing, had brought about the crisis: excessive restriction of the currency and refusal of reasonable accommodation had aggravated it when it came. The nation had not lost its means of producing wealth, or of providing its members with the means of subsistence.

No sooner were the facts faced, so far as they were then understood, than the height of the crisis had passed. The Bank of England was permitted to issue one pound and two pound notes, the Mint was set to work to coin bullion as rapidly as possible, gold was obtained from abroad in considerable quantities, and by the end of the year, which had begun amid universal content and general jubilation, the despairing people had decided that they might yet be able to meet their losses and pull through. Notwithstanding the enormous scale of the undertakings and commitments in comparison with the population and realised wealth of the Great Britain of that day, the bankruptcies after all were not numerous. The actual loss was not nearly so great as men in their panic had thought. Savings had been swept away to a large extent, and the bitter cry of the small investor, the subdued wail of the widow and the orphan, was heard in the land. But from the economical point of view, and as regarded the interests of the mass of the people, the greatest mischief was caused by the glut of commodities, which Fourier, following the lead of Robert Owen, pointed to as the peculiar feature of this trade crisis in every country affected by it. That glut of commodities was increased by the anxiety of the middle-class and the wealthy to make up by economy for the losses which they had sustained; and men and women were again thrown out of work as before by the fact that their power to produce wealth was being continually enhanced, while they themselves had as little control over the ownership or the distribution of the wealth which they produced as they had over the raw material, machinery, and tools by which through them it was created.

Again, therefore, as a result of causes over which they had no control, Great Britain was overrun by workless people, and disturbances and riots were the rule rather than the exception; for Englishmen had not yet accepted the doctrine that it was their duty to starve in silence and contentment because the managers of modern industry had made fools of themselves. They saw that, no matter how successful the speculations of the well-to-do might have been, the wage-earners would have in nowise benefited from the profits realised; and it seemed to them – this was sixty-seven years ago, and before the schoolmaster was fairly abroad – that they should scarcely be called upon to pay in the shape of starvation and misery for themselves, their wives, and their children, because the ruling classes had staked and lost the national wealth at the international gambling table of finance and commerce. They even went so far as to translate their opinions on this subject into action, were duly shot down, hanged, and imprisoned for their ignorant misconception of the truths of middle-class political economy, and were taught a rude lesson as to the advantages of law and order even to a starving people under modern social conditions.

In the meantime, the Government was carefully considering what seemed to them the far more important question of the regulation of the Bank of England. One pound and two pound notes were now finally given up in England, though their circulation was still permitted in Scotland, and the Bank of England was authorised to establish branches in several of the great provincial cities. It was hoped that these measures would materially lessen the probability of the recurrence of crisis, and would limit its injurious effect if it took place. How far this anticipation was realised will shortly be seen.

The crisis of 1825 had a considerable effect on all the foreign markets which, in some cases, felt the results of it after Great Britain herself had recovered from the shock. English goods, unsaleable at home, were thrown in masses on the foreign markets, depressing prices to a great extent, as the previous rise in England had maintained values. The financial crash which followed, however, though it was felt throughout the civilised world, did not have the same influence as similar disturbances produced later. International financial and commercial relations had not yet become so closely intertwined as they afterwards became, and even the United States, temporarily affected as they were by the outrageous speculation carried on in raw cotton during 1825, experienced nothing which could be called a serious crisis, intimately connected as the interests of the two countries now were.

Those who witnessed the crisis of 1825 and the series of events which led up to it, ought to have been able to prepare for and provide against similar social catastrophes. The early portion of the present century produced many Englishmen, who saw as clearly as did Owen that the increased power to create wealth had become in the hands of the dominant class a direct means for the manufacture of poverty. But, unfortunately, their warnings passed unheeded, the doctrine of non-interference was at this time raised to the level of an indisputable religious dogma, and, consequently, the economical evolution was left to work itself out at the expense of much loss to the country, and of endless suffering to the victims of the system. The truth, of course, being that, though the evils might have been palliated, the form of the development was inevitable.

III. The Crisis of 1836-1839

Great Britain had thus entered upon that series of trade depressions and trade inflations, of confident adventure and utter hopelessness, of "boom" and crisis, which have continued to our own day. It was during these first thirty years of the century that England fully confirmed and extended the position which she had gained during the great war. The first-fruits of all the great inventions fell to her lot, and the fact that these great inventions were brought to bear practically at almost the same time, in many different branches of industry, had a cumulative effect. A complete transformation was being carried out. An agricultural country, with a proportionate amount of native manufactures and a considerable commerce, was being turned into the workshop of the world, and the sea-carrying trade, owing to geographical position as well as naval victories, fell more and more into English hands.

At this period, also, for the first time since the downfall of the monasteries and the neglect to maintain the public roads which ensued thereupon, the internal communications of the island began to receive the attention which they deserved. This was a matter of pressing necessity. It was impossible to transport large quantities of manufactured goods to the seaports at a profit over such roads as those which led from one town in Lancashire and Yorkshire to another at the commencement of the development of the great machine industries. The cotton, wool, silk, and linen manufactures, carried on as they now were by steam-power, required great quantities of coal delivered at the mills at a cheap price; and the iron industry, which had received a tremendous impetus from many quarters, required still more coal and ores delivered at low rates in order to maintain that cheapness which could alone secure the continuance of England's industrial supremacy. Canals, perhaps the cheapest and best means of conveying heavy goods even yet discovered, were the first important improvement made in this direction, and some of the greatest of these works were completed at the end of the eighteenth century, largely contributing to the development of the great cities which they connected with one another,

Turnpike roads constructed on sound principles soon followed, and the work done by the Romans hundreds of years before in this island was done over again, though far less solidly, to meet the exigencies of the new era. Tramways, also, which sometimes appear to us to be one of the methods of conveyance adopted by the present generation, were in common use in all the mining and industrial districts during the first quarter of the present century. Transport was, in fact, making strenuous efforts to keep pace with the exigencies of manufacture, and the appearance of steam vessels on the ocean was evidence to the more clear-sighted that no long time could elapse before the same great power would be applied to locomotion on land. The crisis of 1825 in nowise arrested this necessary development. If the numbers of the unemployed and the miserable condition of the mass of the people constituted, as at this period they unquestionably did, a serious political and social danger for the dominant classes, the cheap labour provided by the ill-paid toil of themselves, their wives, and their children, offered a premium on capitalist experiment in every direction. All the disturbances and riots, all the political discontent and social conspiracy, had little effect upon the steady, economical progress which went on below. The people starved; but production was enhanced and transport was improved in a manner altogether unprecedented. In 1830 the first railway was established in England between Liverpool and Manchester.

In this year, 1830, also, owing to good harvests and the recovery in business from the dulness which succeeded the collapse of 1825, a thorough revival set in so far as the interests of the profit-making classes were concerned. The rate of discount fell away and another period of speculation began with its inevitable accompaniments of inflation and over-trading. In the ten years, from 1821 to 1831, the population of England .and Wales alone increased from 12,000,000 to 14,000,000, though the condition of the working-people presented a sad contrast to the well-being of their forerunners in the first half of the previous century; and the enactment of the New Poor Law of 1834 rendered their prospects more hopeless than ever. In 1835 the Chartist movement took shape in an organised body, and from that date onwards for several years turmoil, rioting, and semi-insurrection pervaded the country.

But all this, though it might slightly impede, could not greatly check the expansion which had commenced a few years before. The year 1836 provided the second of two exceptionally abundant harvests in succession, and, similar causes producing the like effects, 1836 witnessed a recurrence of that mania of speculation and therewith an astounding expansion of confidence and credit which had ended in the crash of 1825. It is unnecessary to enlarge upon the folly of speculators and investors at such periods, unless new features of mania present themselves for analysis and consideration. The memory of investors and men of business is always short, and modern conditions of finance and commerce tend to limit their foresight. Thus each successive generation of ten years produces its fresh crop of needy adventurers and credulous premium-hunters. There is really no necessity to invent new methods: the financial three-card trick and the commercial confidence dodge never fail to attract a new set of victims, and those who perpetrate them successfully, instead of undergoing imprisonment, attain to the highest positions in the city, society, and politics.

Untaught by the lessons of the previous crash, the banks

again did all in their power to push to the extreme the eager desire to embark on new ventures and to carry commercial initiative far beyond the farthest bounds of prudence. By the Bank Act of 1826, banking companies could be formed with the power to issue notes, under certain conditions, of a denomination not less than £5. In the first seven years after the promulgation of this Act, thirty-four such banks of issue were set on foot, and in the three following years, to the end of 1835,about the same number. "In the year 1836, speculation had again reached such a pitch that forty-two new banks of issue were established which, with their branches, gave a total of fully two hundred, and taking into consideration other credit establishments and their branch banks, there were no fewer than 670 such institutions on foot with about thirty-seven thousand shareholders; and of these three-fourths issued their own notes." During these years, both the Bank of England and the other banks had issued paper largely in excess of the amounts previously in circulation. But now in the spring of 1836, the Bank of England, as in 1825, began to reduce its note issue, and was forced in view of the drain for gold which had set in to America to raise its rate of discount. Thereupon, the banks of issue, instead of following the Bank of England's lead, issued fifty per cent. more notes than before, thus rendering the directors' action to protect their gold reserve from depletion almost nugatory. Hence arose an expansion of credit which speedily gave rise to a glut. A great bank in Ireland suddenly failed, and a run commenced on the provincial banks of the South of England which threatened to end as disastrously as the similar run in 1825, seeing that the banks of issue held at this time but a sixth part of their note circulation in specie. This time, however, the Bank of England came to the rescue of one of the great northern banks, and a crash was staved off.

Now, however, became apparent the close connection of the English commercial and financial markets with those of the United States which, then and ever since, has rendered it inevitable that an industrial or financial crisis in the one country should more or less seriously affect the other. At this time, 1836-39, the United States were still, economically speaking, a dependency of Great Britain, though more than sixty years had passed since the Declaration of Independence. North America, in fact, stood to England in much the same relation that the Australian Colonies do now. The Great Republic supplied the Lancashire mills almost exclusively with cotton, as Australia now supplies Bradford, Huddersfield, and other cities with wool. In like manner, also, the United States, both as a Federal Government and as independent States, looked to this country for loans to develop their immeasurable resources.

The dependence of the English cotton industry upon the United States for its supply of raw material had already in 1824 and 1825 given rise to a vast deal of speculation which rose to such a point as to, assume the dimensions of a great modern "corner" in that staple. Then, however, as at a much later date, during the Civil War, it was discovered that when the price exceeded a certain figure, other countries were glad of the opportunity to supplement the deficiency and to benefit by English custom. During the interval between 1825 and 1836, the United States had entered upon a career of false banking based to a large extent upon fictitious land sales and backed up by loans incurred in Great Britain. From 1832 onwards, a period of wild speculation had commenced, which the banks as usual had helped to extend and intensify by an excessive issue of paper money, amounting in the year 1837 to £90,000,000 for a population of about 18,000,000; an inflation which individual capitalists carried yet further by raising loans on their private property and businesses in England.

In spite of the warnings of President Jackson, this dangerous system was pushed to the extreme. In vain was the extravagance, corruption, and swindling denounced by those who saw whither all this must lead. Paper money in excess seemed an easy way for all to make fortunes at once, and none would listen to reason so long as the universal prosperity seemed unshaken. In short, the old story of all such periods was retold on the other side of the Atlantic. The price of land and commodities, the rents of houses and the wages of labour, all rose together, and endless new enterprises were undertaken, numberless new houses were built. Any difficulty in high places was met by still further loans at high rates of interest in London and Amsterdam. There seemed literally no limit to the length to which things might be pushed, as there was assuredly no restriction put upon the action of the banks. No one seems to have imagined that the upset of all this extravagance and folly could come from England, which had been helping by her loans to breed this exaggerated confidence.

No telegraph then existed to keep the more wary on the alert as to the coming change. But the rise in the rate of discount which followed opened their eyes, and the crash which ensued was on a scale of truly New World magnitude. When credit first gave way the whole of the American banks suspended specie payments, and eventually in 1837, 618 banks, and in 1839, no fewer than 959 banks, failed. Notes became worthless, loans remained unpaid, advances were not to be had, bankruptcies seemed to become the rule in trade rather than the exception. The records of the period show that the Americans themselves felt for a time almost hopeless of any speedy recovery. The advocates of "soft money" had had for the moment their fill of it.

The influence of such a crisis as this in America reacted most injuriously upon Great Britain. Those who had made advances on American produce at high prices – and they had been made on a stupendous scale – saw no way of recovering their money. Those who had lent on lands or other estates, or had invested in the shares of American banks, saw their fortunes swept away by a stroke. American credit in England received a blow from which it took a long time to revive, and English literature was enriched by some scathing diatribes against American rascality and breach of faith. Not until 1839 was the full extent of the disaster appreciated, when a series of failures occurred far in excess of the average; the gold reserve in the Bank of England fell to little over two millions and a half; and unless exceptional measures had been resorted to, another financial crisis of a still worse character than that of 1837 would have followed the raising of the bank rate of discount to 6 per cent. No wonder that this year, 1839, looked black for the working-classes, and that revolutionary propaganda made rapid progress among the ill-paid or workless people. So bad was the lot of the workers that the "Condition of England " question was the topic most seriously discussed in the Cabinet as in the street.

Yet throughout all this anarchy and apparent impoverishment, the well-to-do classes, it cannot be too often repeated, were becoming steadily richer, and the wealth of the country, as well as its power to produce more wealth, constantly and continuously grew. Exports and imports mounted upwards, the fluctuations bearing but a small proportion to the bulk of the whole. Public buildings, private mansions, great factories, vast warehouses, public works calling for huge capital expenditure, were all being erected at the very time when the state of large portions of the population occasioned grave anxiety to the statesman, the economist, and the philanthropist alike. Within a period of thirty years the annual rental of real property in England and Wales alone increased by £40,000,000: the tonnage of vessels sailing under the English flag was six-fold greater than it had been at the beginning of the century.

In agriculture the advance was not so rapid as in manufacture or in transport; but even there the increased power of production was very marked. The country was still almost entirely dependent on its own resources for the supply of wheat, and that supply had increased by 44,000,000 of bushels a year in the course of forty years, though the agricultural population had increased to a very small extent.

But with these unmistakable facts before them, and made day by day the subject of vigorous comments by able writers and speakers on the question from the point of view of the producers, the Government and the House of Commons confined themselves to tinkering with the banking system. Now it is quite unnecessary to say that when banks are carefully managed on a sound basis the danger of a financial and industrial crisis assuming unmanageable proportions, owing to undue and absurd inflation of the currency and consequent unreasoning speculation, is much lessened: But banking, after all, is only a convenient method of conducting one portion of the machinery of production and exchange under the capitalist system. So long as one class carries on the business of the country, solely for profit, and is prevented by the very law of its being from ordering matters in such wise that a proper harmony is established between expenditure on permanent works and on day-to-day business, it is quite impossible that the soundest methods of banking that can be established should do more than work the credit system with the least obstruction that circumstances will admit of. The experience of the English banks, and more particularly of the Bank of England during the crises up to the year 1839, had shown that the mischiefs, unfortunately the unrecognised mischiefs, of a method of creating wealth which refused to permit any control to those who actually created it, might be and had been much aggravated by mistakes in banking.

Let the Bank of England, it was said, be placed on such a footing that excessive issues of paper currency would be checked; let due warning be given of the approach of stringency by the reduction of the necessary reserve and all would be well. English trade was at this time becoming more and more a trade of borrowed capital. That is to say, men were looking to the banks to provide the bulk of the capital with which they traded at a rate of interest guided by the market rate, of which one and generally the crucial criterion was the bank rate, their own capital providing only a margin for possible loss. Joint Stock Banks were then in their infancy, and the importance of the Bank of England relating to the banking world of England and to the money market at large was much greater in every way than it is to-day. It was natural, therefore, for those who did not look below the surface to imagine that if the Bank of England was ordered aright, the probability of the recurrence of disastrous crises would be materially reduced if not moved altogether.

Without going at length into the history of the Bank of England, or discussing fully over again the much-debated Bank Charter Act of 1844, it is interesting to observe the steps which were taken by the government to remedy the evils of excessive note issue and over-confidence. The Bank of England holds quite an exceptional position as a bank. It is not a State bank like the Bank of France, nor is it together a private or Joint Stock Bank, seeing that has a practical monopoly of Government business, and, which is more important, is regarded by the majority even of business people, who ought to know better, as in some sort a State institution. In theory, and to a large extent in practice, the Bank of England is a bank like other banks, accepting deposits either with or without interest, and lending out those deposits again to other customers who need them in the shape of advances on bills or easily saleable securities at a margin. But this sort of business calls for a reserve to be used in case of panic; otherwise in a moment of stringency when everybody wants money there would not be cash enough to meet current demands.

Now, the Bank of England holds not only its own reserve to meet national demands for specie payments, but also the bullion to meet foreign payments. Moreover, the other banks, instead of keeping their own reserves, keep them in the Bank of England; and to the Bank of England alone can bankers and men of business resort in periods of great financial disturbance to obtain advances on Consols or other first-rate securities, which, though in ordinary times easily convertible into cash by means of sales or loans upon them, cannot be dealt with in the same way when all at the same moment are panic-stricken in their anxiety to obtain legal tender, and thus provide the means to pay their day-to-day liabilities. Of the attempts of the Bank to keep a reserve, and to manage a foreign drain after the resumption of specie payments in 1819, "a more miserable history can hardly be found." So says a great authority, and the brief survey of the facts given in the foregoing pages certainly bears out this strong condemnation.

Instead of showing that sagacity, promptitude, and foresight which the public believe the heads of the City must be possessed of, the Directors of the Bank of England were just as silly as anybody else. It was to provide securities against the incapacity of the ablest financiers of the country that Peel's Bank Act was passed into law. By this Act the Bank of England was divided into two parts – the department for the issue of notes and the banking department – which are really quite separate, though they remained, and still remain, under one roof. In the issue department, Bank of England notes, which are legal tender, can only be issued to the extent of £15,000,000 on Government securities, £11,015,100 of this being a Government debt. Any further issue of notes must be represented by gold coin and bullion in the hands of the Bank to the full amount, no issue against silver being permitted. That is the full extent to which the Bank is by law permitted to go.

Now, wonderfully as the amount of gold necessary to do a given amount of business has been reduced by the modern development of cheques and the clearinghouse, gold or absolutely sound notes must be obtained in sufficient quantity in times of difficulty to stem the current of panic, and enable trade to go on again as speedily as may be. Bad as the management of the Bank of England was from certain points of view in 1825 and in 1837, it can scarcely be questioned that the issue of notes which were absolute legal tender, but were not fully represented by bullion, did circumscribe the range of the mischief occasioned by those disastrous crises. But under the Act of 1844 such action by the Directors was no longer possible. The two departments were severed, and the one might be denuded of coin and bullion while the other had a superfluity, which it could not by law supply in the only way then possible to restrict the panic, namely, by issuing more notes. Thus a sudden drain produced a twofold effect.

In this case, as in many others of a like kind, the theorists saw farther than the practical men. While the bankers and City people approved of the Bank Act, with its division of departments, and rigid restriction of the note issue on securities to £15,000,000, such writers as Mill, Tooke, and others predicted that on the first serious crisis the Act, owing to the inelasticity which it caused, would be found to be unworkable, and would have to be suspended. As will be seen by what followed, they proved perfectly right; and it may be said even to-day that the Bank Act of 1844 is only maintained because, at the critical moment, everybody knows it will be treated as a dead letter. This strange sort of fatalism in business seems to be worthy of the singular arrangement by which a body of men who are not bankers, and whose personal and business interests may any day be opposed to the real interests of the Bank, are placed as Directors in control of that which is the most important banking institution of the greatest commercial country in the world.

It is not necessary to know much about the details of banking, or to master the theory on which the Bank Act of 1844 is founded, in order to understand the practical working of stringency in producing panic. Nearly all manufacturers and traders carry on their business now, as has been said, on borrowed capital. To meet their own bills for raw material or goods, they must discount other people's bills. So long as the bank rate keeps at a point which enables them to borrow in the open market, that is, to discount their own and other people's paper at say four or five, or even perhaps six per cent., they can make a reasonable profit on their own small capital, which forms the narrow basis of all this great edifice of business. But when, owing to a farther rise in the bank rate, and the stringency following thereupon, bill-brokers and bankers are more anxious to protect themselves than to provide for their customers, even those manufacturers, merchants, and traders who can still get accommodation by paying for it find that their margin of profit is swept away, and their own capital locked up in the business is actually threatened. A prolonged squeeze in such conditions would force half the business world into liquidation. For goods and commodities, however valuable they may be, represent to their owners no available means of meeting their engagements in cash, and cash or its equivalent alone is what is needed to enable the machine to pass its dead points; nor will the best securities supply the need of the moment, seeing that cases have occurred in which the Bank of England hesitated to advance upon Consols.

The crisis of 1836-1839, commonly spoken of as the crisis of 1837, was therefore the last which occurred under the old banking conditions. From 1841 onwards the system has remained the same in form so far as the Bank of England is concerned.

IV. The Crisis of 1847

England had now commenced that period of railway construction and Free Trade which raised the commercial prosperity of the country to a higher point than ever. There were those who imagined – and they were by no means the most foolish people in the country – that this improvement in communications, followed as it was in 1846 by a cheapening of the main staple of food by the removal of all Protective duties on wheat, would do away once for all with starvation and distress, and bring classes together as they had never yet been combined. As a consequence, crises would in future be unknown, and trade would progress inevitably upwards with increasing benefit to the whole population. But the way in which Englishmen set to work to supply themselves with railroads was in itself a marked instance of the anarchy then prevailing in regard to what constitute public interests. At first when railways were in the experimental stage, and this stage lasted, so far as public opinion was affected, much longer than is commonly supposed, it was perhaps advisable, in the then condition of development, that no direct steps should be taken by the Government to control or administer the projected lines, When, however, it became apparent that nothing short of a complete revolution in the entire system of internal transport was being brought about, it was certainly the duty of Parliament to adopt such measures as would restrict waste and prevent the reckless gambling which followed so soon as it was found that railway construction was likely to prove profitable.

It is always impossible for the capitalists of any country to maintain permanently an equilibrium between the amount expended on works of permanent utility, but of slow return in the shape of profit, and the extent of the funds which should be used to carry on business of more immediate practical usefulness. But when a mania for some new form of undertaking seizes upon the investing public, then the savings of the community are too often utterly thrown away upon hopeless enterprises or squandered in constructing works for which there is no real need at the time. This was certainly the case in regard to the era of railway construction. The railway system was "rushed" by speculators and promoters, as the gold-fields were afterwards rushed by the workers. It was a time of furious competition for fresh enterprises. Incompatible schemes jostled one another for precedence. Concession-hunting, regardless of the real value of the enterprise for which the Act was to be obtained, was everywhere the order of the day. People who could ill afford to lose joined in the chase, scraping together every farthing they could rake up, not for the sake of carrying out a useful undertaking, but for the sake of the premium which they hoped to obtain on their shares from someone else. The working capital of business was diverted from its natural province to hurry on the development more rapidly than ever.

Parliament, it is true, stepped in to limit to some extent, by more stringent regulations and detailed requirements, the unreasoning demands for new charters. But this had little effect. The most tremendous efforts were made to hurry forward the completion of reports, and estimates, and plans, and evidence of traffic and public utility. It was indeed a time of stress and strain. All the records of the period prove that the eagerness displayed reached the pitch of positive lunacy. Half-a-dozen or more schemes were proposed for each of the possible routes, and as many more for those which were manifestly hopeless from the first. Each promoter was far more anxious to crush his rivals than to ensure the soundness of his own enterprise. All were in the most desperate haste to put in their demands before the appointed time for closing the list of applications. If half the proposed lines had been carried out, Great Britain would have been gridironed from one end to another with railways, and ordinary traffic would have been rendered impossible. Engineers, draftsmen, lithographers, engravers, and, above all, lawyers, had more work than they could do, paid for at rates far in excess of any that they had previously been able to command. Landowners who opposed and landowners who favoured railways alike asked prices for their land quite beyond anything which it could have realised in a free market. The cost of construction was thus enormously enhanced in the case of successful competitors for any given time; and the people of England are actually paying to-day, in the shape of excessive fares, for the privilege of that ruinous competition, which has only resulted in a monstrous monopoly.

The number of projected railways was, indeed, outside of the limits of reason, and the mileage to which the royal assent was given, though the distances to be traversed seem small in these days of Atlantic and Pacific, and Siberian Railways, was out of all proportion to the capacities of that date, or to the capital available for purposes of construction. On the one day of the 16th July, 1845, no fewer than 05 railway bills received the royal assent, which involved the construction of 600 miles of railway, costing at the lowest estimate upwards of £13,000,000. In the same session of Parliament, 678 projects were submitted, and of these 136, with a mileage of 1,142 miles, involving a capital outlay of nearly £26,000,000, were sanctioned by Parliament. In the course of a single month calls were made on shareholders in home and foreign railways to the extent of £5,227,725. During the years 1845-47 no less than £90,000,000 were spent on railway building. For these, it must be remembered, were the days when Hudson was the Railway King, and people of the highest position and culture were grovelling at the feet of the vulgar potentate, in order to share in the vast wealth which he was assumed to be the master of.

Such an enormous sinking of capital as this on works of permanent utility but of slow return, such a whirl of speculation in shares as followed, must have resulted in a crisis sooner or later. But as Herr Max Wirth truly says, had a good harvest secured the people cheap food, had the raw materials of the chief industries remained at a moderate price, thus enabling the factories to continue the work of production unchecked, and thus to increase the quantity of their output which could find a market, the danger might have passed over without more serious disturbance, and even the worst features of the crisis itself might have possibly been avoided. As it was, however, on the top of all this railway development came a succession of failures of the potato crop in Ireland, a short cotton crop in America and bad harvests in England. Raw materials, instead of being cheap, were very dear, and the prices of the necessaries of life rose two and threefold. Workers were discharged on all hands in England, while millions dependent on one uncertain staple of food were starving in Ireland, and all the improvement in the external trade which had been established could not make amends for the utter collapse in the home markets.

Natural causes conspired this time with the artificial mismanagement to intensify the crisis. The necessity for importing grain on a large scale to meet the prevailing distress was one of the causes which brought the agitation for the repeal of the Corn Laws to a successful issue in 1846. A great speculation in grain had also begun which tended to complicate matters. Thus, already in 1846, there were all and more than usually marked symptoms of an approaching crisis in industry and finance. But the directors of the Bank of England were no more capable of discerning the signs of the times after the enactment of the Bank Charter Act of 1844 than they were before. Once more, by their policy, they helped to fan the speculation, and by maintaining their rate of discount at the low point of 2 per cent. and then 3 per cent., prepared the way for the tremendous drain of gold which set in during the early months of 1847, and scared the whole business community.

The heavy fall in the price of wheat which tumbled in four months from 102s. to 48s. the quarter, though very advantageous to the people at large, brought about one failure after another among grain houses which had not anticipated any such sudden change. In October, the bank rate of discount was 8 per cent, and Consols had gone down from 94 in January, 1847, to 79 in that month. Railway shares fell 15 to 25 per cent., bills could scarcely be discounted at any price, respectable houses were closing their doors by the dozen, workmen were being discharged in every direction, 2,500 navvies being left workless by the contractors for the London and North Western Railway alone. Tens of thousands of workers were, in fact, out of employment and starving, and the condition of the people during the winter seemed likely to be worse than ever; while, what was taking place already in Ireland, and what followed in that awful winter of 1847, has never been forgotten or forgiven by Irishmen in any part of the world.

It was at this juncture, October, 1847, that the worthlessness of the Bank Act of 1844 in time of crisis was first made manifest to the world. Utter carelessness was, as usual, followed by unreasoning panic. As the gold was drained away to meet foreign demands, the directors were forced by the conditions of their charter to lessen the accommodation which they could give at the very moment when the need for such accommodation was most pressing, and nothing short of the most liberal extension of credit to those who could reasonably demand it could, by any possibility, check the panic. The bank rate stood at 8 per cent., and before the Bank Act was suspended and the directors were permitted to issue notes in excess of the £15,000,000 allowed by law without holding gold against them, the banking department was actually reduced to less than £2,000,000. The bank must have stopped payment so far as the banking department was concerned, unless what was virtually bankruptcy had been declared and the Bank Act had been suspended. This suspension itself, though it improved matters, did not at once end the crisis, which dragged on for fully three months more. Confidence had been immediately shaken, and the lack of coin tended to lengthen the period of inevitable distrust.

By degrees, as the memorable year 1848 approached, confidence began to be re-established, and the bank rate gave evidence, by its steady reduction, that the season of panic was over and that only a sort of reasonable mistrust in some quarters survived.

Already the record is becoming almost monotonous in its similarity. The circumstances, indeed, change; but the blunders are repeated and the follies reproduce themselves with an unvarying regularity. New methods of production are discovered and applied. Straightway, they are pushed to such an extent without consideration or foresight, that, though the few become rich, the many are fearfully impoverished and suffer more from social and economical perturbations than from any natural misfortune. An energetic people, with an unbounded territory around them, begin to develop its resources in earnest, and again carry the process to such a pitch as to be incompatible with the system of profit under which they are working, and the methods of banking attendant thereon. Another collapse follows, affecting populations on both sides of the Atlantic. A means of land transportation, more rapid and advantageous than any before known, is adopted in the wealthiest and most civilised country in the world. The first effect of what should be an advantage to all the inhabitants is first to turn the heads of the entire money-manipulating portion of the population, to force on a mania for speculation of a most injurious kind, and, eventually, in conjunction with other causes, to throw once more thousands of people out of work and into misery and starvation. So little do the governing classes and mercantile men appreciate the situation that they themselves set on foot, with a view to lessen the evils arising from these recurring periods of break-down, a banking arrangement which can only be saved from landing the whole country in bankruptcy by declaring its own bankruptcy just before this actually occurs.

But in this crisis of 1847 we can trace more clearly than heretofore the international and almost world-wide nature of these commercial convulsions. Paris, Amsterdam, Frankfort, and New York, all felt the counterstroke of this primarily English crisis of 1847, and the great political revolutionary movement of 1848 on the Continent, which in part assumed a socialistic shape, was preceded by the shock of the economic earthquake that had its centre of disturbance in London. Bankruptcies, not only of trading firms, but of industrial concerns, followed. The same causes which had occasioned the upset in English business, outside the great railway mania, were now manifestly at work on the Continent. Banks were compelled to raise their rates of interest on advances to protect themselves; and that mutual interchange of compliments, in the shape of unloading securities by turns on the various international financial exchanges, became henceforward a permanent portion of the general system of finance. The next great crisis will exhibit this solidarity of markets in a yet more striking manner.

Meanwhile, a sort of law of periodicity was beginning to be traced. Men had not yet begun to talk of ten years as the trade cycle, but that ups and downs of trade were to be looked for as a necessary accompaniment of the great extension of modern industry and finance was a growing opinion. In England, at any rate, 1815, 1825, 1837 and 1847, induced all connected with business to regard similar phenomena of inflation as the almost certain forerunners of a similar crash in due time.

V. The Crisis of 1857

The ten year period from 1847 to 1857 is, perhaps, the most noteworthy period in the history of the civilised world, since the discovery of America and the rounding of the Cape of Good Hope entirely changed the outlook for European commerce. It is true that no geographical discoveries were made at all comparable in importance to those which astounded mankind at the end of the fifteenth and beginning of the sixteenth century, neither were there any similar conquests to those of Mexico and Peru to record. But the development of railways, the increase of steam vessels, the great gold discoveries of California, Australia, and New Zealand, had practically the effect of bringing new worlds into connection with the old as well as of stimulating the old-settled communities to extraordinary efforts.

Close upon the heels of the crisis of 1847, came the revolutionary shake of 1848, which, notwithstanding the Chartist scare in London on April 10th, had less effect on England than on any other country. In this year, 1848, also began that wholesale emigration of the Irish people to America which has done so much to build up the wealth of the great republic of the United States. In 1847, gold was discovered in California, and in 1849 began that remarkable rush of the most active and adventurous spirits among the young men of Europe and America to the new lands of the golden fleece in the Pacific Ocean, which has had ever since such a great influence on the commerce of the globe. New life was given to enterprise in every direction. Gold-mining is of itself necessarily a wasteful and unproductive employment of labour and capital. For gold has little real utility as an article of human consumption, and is only useful in quantity as a medium of exchange and standard of value in regard to other products of human labour.

Nevertheless, the direct and indirect effect of these great gold discoveries was to give a tremendous impetus to trade.

Before these discoveries a general shrinkage of prices had set in along the whole range of commodities, and as this was partly due to scarcity of gold, speculations were even indulged in as to the necessity for the abandonment of gold and the substitution of silver as the standard of value and most important currency even in the wealthiest country. The shrinkage of prices was and is due to far more complicated causes than the abundance or scarcity of the precious metals; but in this particular case it is probable that the quantity of gold in circulation or available, say in the year 1848, was insufficient to maintain the old level of prices as measured in gold, and that, but for the new discoveries, some mechanical difficulties would have been encountered in the endeavour to accommodate business to the lower plane of prices. But, with the opening up of the new gold fields, all fear of change in that direction was at an end. Gold could now be raised for a time at less labour-cost than ever before in the history of human society; a higher in place of a lower level of prices was on the average established; and, as all the gold was raised in countries which were inhabited by English-speaking people and with which English traders then had most advantageous relations, England was the nation which benefited in the first instance by the extraordinarily rapid development of California and Australia in the period with which we are dealing.

Thanks to the influx of gold which now commenced on a scale quite unprecedented, there was no difficulty in meeting the demands of the Governments of France and England for currency during the Crimean War; whereas, but for this, it is the opinion of those best able to judge that the Bank of England would have been forced to suspend specie payments as it did from 1797 to 1819. The gold imports from America and Australia removed all fear of any such suspension. Following upon the discoveries and the emigration came, as has been said, an enormous demand for English commodities, so that the crisis of 1847 and the political disturbances of 1848 were soon forgotten in the unexampled revival of trade which ensued. In 1851, the lookout was already so favourable that, at the first great International Exhibition held in that year, there was a general outburst of mutual congratulations, and some actually thought, and many still more foolishly said, that the era of peace and goodwill among men had set in, that wars henceforth would be impossible, and that those present at the Crystal Palace in Hyde Park were unconsciously celebrating the inauguration of the domination of industrialism as against that of militarism all over the world.

The mere fact that such a successful International Exhibition should have been held in London in 1851 was, of course, an evidence of the manner in which the various nations were being knit together in one sense by the bonds of trade, as well as a proof that the means of communication and transport were vastly improving, and abridging distance to an unprecedented degree. But the Exhibition itself did but serve to intensify that national and international competition and anxiety to capture new markets which lie at the root of all the industrial anarchy and crisis that produce periodically the terrible results which no pretence of peaceful intentions can alter.

But from 1851 onwards, until the Crimean War began, such was the prosperity in trade that there was really some ground for imagining that the sanguine prophecies of the Cobdenite school would be fulfilled. The output of gold, and with it the demand for English goods for America and then Australia, continually increased. Continental trade developed in almost equal ratio, and that German emigration to the United States began which was destined to assume even greater proportions than the emigration from Ireland, and to have a yet more beneficial influence on the fortunes of the Great Republic.

Now, too, that export of grain from America to Europe, and particularly to England, began to attain a magnitude which surpassed even the old export of. cotton. The comparatively cheap food thus provided, even with a rapidly increasing population, enabled the capitalists to realise enormous profits, and such was the demand for English products that the nation was able to bear the bad harvest of 1853, and to pass through the Crimean War, with its vast expenditure and fearful mismanagement, almost uninjured. There were short lulls in the forward rush, but, on the whole, there was no check in this long sweep of wealth-creation for the civilised peoples, or rather for the upper and middle classes of those peoples. England, as the chief capitalist country, benefited most by the impetus given to production and commerce, but other nations had now entered upon the same stage of development, and on the Continent and in the United States riches were piled up to an extent previously undreamed of.

For, while gold was pouring into England at the average rate for a series of years of upwards of £25,000,000 a-year, and the total supply of gold in the world was increased by fully one-third in the course of nine years, the demand for capital was also growing in every direction. Improved methods of production, the provision of larger and more rapid steam-vessels for the transport of the masses of raw material and commodities to and fro, the continuous construction of railways, not only in England and the United States, but all over the continent of Europe, gave English capitalists most profitable outlets for their accumulations; while every new district opened and every fresh market conquered, tended to swell the volume of external trade. Home trade also received a progressive impulse from the completion and extension of the main lines of railway, which was another feature of this time of amazing development. It is stated that in the five years from 1846 to 1850, not less than £150,000,000 were spent on English railways, and in an astonishingly short space of time the island was covered with the new roads.

For the slack time in this branch of the new development lasted for little more than a few months after the crisis of 1847, and by the year 1855 there were 8,300 miles of railway, nearly all of them with double lines of rails, opened in Great Britain. We are even now, perhaps, too near to these years of sudden expansion, and also too much accustomed ourselves to the methods which brought it about, fully to appreciate the contrast between what had been and what was. But it is safe to say that a still greater transformation was wrought in the general condition and commercial power of England at this date than had been effected even between the end of the eighteenth century and 1837. All the effects of the far-reaching revolution in the methods of production and transportation seemed to be realised at once, and the shrinkage of the planet, as represented by the comparative accessibility of its parts, became strikingly apparent.

Moreover, the influence of the gold discoveries by no means stopped short at the multiplication of the precious metals, and the consequent temporary ease in the money market and inflation in various directions. Those who went forth as gold-diggers soon turned many of them to the production of other wealth. California and the West of America generally, as well as Australia and New Zealand, found that labour expended on the growing of wool and cereals, meat and fruits, represented in the long run a far more certain return than its precarious and economically wasteful employment on mining. It was not so much the gold production itself as the development of new territories to which this gold production led that really increased the wealth of the world. It is indeed more than doubtful whether the quantity of labour expended directly and indirectly in the search for gold would not have been better repaid, even to the miners themselves, by work in other directions. The waste of labour in mere shaft-sinking, which brings no greater benefit to the unlucky prospector than digging a hole and filling it up again, can only be fully appreciated by those who have observed the process going on under their eyes; while the cost of conveying material and food to some of the distant diggings, before railways or even roads were made, rendered the ordinary standard of life of a digger on the gold-fields as dear as the most luxurious cookery in a city in Europe could possibly have been.

Thus no sooner were the richer and more accessible alluvial deposits exhausted, the precious metal having then to be sought farther up country or extracted from the quartz by the expenditure of much capital and labour in sinking to considerable depths and the provision of elaborate machinery for crushing and amalgamation, than it was found that in many cases even gold itself can be bought too dear. The excessive outlay on these gambling ventures, therefore, tended to help on the crisis which other events were preparing.

A careful survey of the countries which now formed a portion of the great world-market shows that the United States, more even than Great Britain, was likely to benefit by this rising cycle of trade and the construction of railways. Improved communications were above all needed to develop the marvellous resources of the vast territory which, though it had become more densely populated since the crash of 1837, was still, at the beginning of the upward movement of 1849, in great need of further immigration from Europe. This immigration, as has been said, was supplied at first from Ireland, and then more slowly, but more surely, from Germany, England, and Scandinavia. Apart from the savings which these invaluable labourers brought with them, they also, by the outlet which their industry provided, and the vast wealth which it was at once recognised that their settlement in so rich an agricultural and mineral region must create, induced European capitalists, in spite of their earlier experience, to embark in American ventures on a larger scale than ever.

As England ceased to produce sufficient wheat for her needs, America came forward to supply the want; and during the Crimean War, the people of the United States derived great profit from the quantities of food which they were able to furnish without difficulty. The enormous production and export of food stuffs, in the shape of wheat, maize, etc., added to the old staples of rice and cotton, grown by the slave-owners of the South, turned North America into a huge factory farm, to supply Europe with grain and raw material. In return she took great quantities of manufactured articles of all kinds. An increase of wealth per head of population was thus established, unequalled even in Great Britain, and at this time the wealth was far more evenly distributed than it is today throughout the Northern States, whose political and industrial preponderance in the Union was becoming more marked every year. Republican America, notwithstanding the institution of slavery, was regarded throughout Europe as the land of promise, and the tidings of her prosperity and rapid expansion encouraged the continuous immigration which still further extended her wealth and prosperity. Here, as elsewhere, the apparent wealth represented by the output of gold tended to increase the activity of the production of real wealth; and, here as elsewhere, excessive speculation, fraud, luxury, and outrageous extravagance followed; while too great a proportion of the savings of the well-to-do were again expended on works of permanent utility but slow return, such as railways, for the gain even of the capitalist class.

Up to the spring of 1857, with the blindness which is peculiar to such cases, no one saw any sign of the approaching crash. The Americans took good care to let all the world know of their wonderful progress. "A report, published at the commencement of 1857, stated that the year 1856 had given results of which the past had afforded no example. Enormous advance had been made; the cultivation of new territories, the produce of harvests, the extension of factories, the exploitation of mines, the exports and imports, the carrying trade, shipbuilding, the railway returns, the spread and improvement of cities – in a word, anything which can tend to the enrichment of a great country, has received such a vigorous impulse that, since the Declaration of Independence, not even the most far-seeing men had ventured to predict the attainment of such a high degree of prosperity.

"And, as a matter of fact, statistics seemed to justify this opinion. In the clearing-house affairs of New York there was an increase of 1,300,000,000 dollars or 30 per cent. The imports and exports of New York had risen in 1856 to the extent of 33 per cent., and the railway traffic from 20 to 30 per cent. Not less than 17,600,000 acres of State territories had been sold, an extent equal to that of Belgium and Holland put together. In addition, the Railway Congress had ceded to such States as later wished to build lines 21,700,000 acres of land, which makes up in all 39,700,000 acres, or about a third of entire France. Agricultural and industrial production had kept pace with the progress noted above: it had risen in 1856 to 2,600,000,000 dollars, that is, had increased threefold in fifteen years. Immovable property was estimated at over 11,000,000,000 dollars, and the population at 27,000,000. The public debt had been reduced in this year by 25 per cent., that is, to 30,000,000 dollars. The length of telegraph lines exceeded 50,000 English miles. The railways, of which there were upwards of 21,000 miles in 1855, were extended to 24,000 miles in 1856, and the following table shows their cost to have been the cheapest in the world:

		English Miles	Cost in Dollars	Cost per Mile
United States	(1856)	24195	846,825,000	$35,000.00
Great Britain	(1855)	8297	1,487,916,420	$179,000
France	(1856)	4,038	616,118,995	$152,000

Germany	(1855)	3,213	228,000,000	$71,000
Prussia	(1855)	1,290	145,000,000	$63,000
Belgium	(1855)	1005	98,500,000	$30,000

Such a balance sheet had never before been drawn for any people, and it is not surprising that many heads were turned by it, or that the majority even of cool-headed men of business thought that, based as it was upon agricultural production, and accompanied by a great increase of population and a simultaneous reduction of the State debt, there was no reason to fear any sudden overthrow. Nevertheless, the collapse was all ready. The very increase of prosperity, not only in agriculture, but in manufacture, the development of the iron and coal of Pennsylvania, as well as the manufactures of New England; the astounding railway construction, on which the whole nation prided itself, all prepared the way for the crisis which was close at hand. Some of the causes which rendered that crisis so disastrous were common to other countries with the United States; but the banking system of America tended to make it worse when it came than elsewhere, as its great agricultural resources rendered the revival more rapid.

At this time American banks were lending in excess of all reason, and on the 22nd of August, 1857, the total loans of the New York banks actually exceeded by 12,000,000 dollars the total amount of specie, notes, and deposits in their coffers. At the same time, however, the note issue was fairly sound in relation to the specie held against them. "The suspension of the banks which soon followed arose, not from the inconvertibility of notes, but from the wholesale withdrawal of deposits." But in America also was seen the bad side of the gold discoveries. Men forgot that gold will no more feed or clothe or house labourers than an issue of assignats. Gold is in America, as everywhere else, only a representation of value and a means of exchange. But the superfluity of gold misled men of business into imagining that an increase of currency, or an accumulation of the precious metals in reserve, meant that the country was really wealthier to that extent and yet more. Thus, on the one hand, the rash policy of the banks of deposit in discounting beyond reason, and, on the other, the abundance of the precious metals, deceived the world of business as to what was in store for it. This state of things was accompanied by the usual chicane and rascality, on which it is not necessary to dwell.

But the main causes of the collapse were the same as ever; the incapacity of the heads of the capitalist system to regulate the amount of capital expended on the development of different branches of industry. Over-speculation in every direction was accompanied also by a tremendous accumulation of goods in the warehouses, in anticipation of the higher prices which seemed certain from the success hitherto attained in disposing of commodities. Much of the goods thus stored had been obtained upon credit from Europe. At the first serious shake, therefore, down must come the entire edifice on both sides of the Atlantic. At the beginning of August, a time of year when the city of New York is out of season, and men of business are as far as possible away on their holidays, the crisis commenced with a few small failures. A week later money was so tight, owing to withdrawals of deposits, and the hoarding of gold and silver, that business was carried on with difficulty. On the 24th of August a great bank of high repute suspended payment. Then the panic began in grim earnest. Bankers, merchants, financiers, and stock-jobbers all lost their heads together. The banks restricted their advances and called in their loans; the rate of discount ran up to 25 per cent.; bank shares, railway shares, and bonds were unsaleable; and bank failures, mercantile failures, and traders' bankruptcies were rather the rule than the exception.

By the month of October business was at a standstill, and the most necessary trade could scarcely be carried on, though the warehouses, as usual at such periods, were glutted with goods that nobody could buy. The rate of interest ran up to 60, to 100, per cent. Nobody could meet his bills. Utter consternation set in, aggravated by the great excitability which Americans evince at such times. A run on the soundest banks began such as had never before been experienced. The run began on the 9th. By the evening of the 13th, eighteen banks had come down with an indebtedness to depositors of about 21,000,000 dollars. Remittances could no longer be made to the West, and a fall in prices of commodities from 10 to 35 per cent. had taken place all along the line. Fourteen great railway companies, whose names are well known in London, such as the Illinois Central, the Philadelphia, and Reading, the New York and Lake Eric, and many more also suspended payment.

The influence of the crisis upon industry was as bad as it was upon trade, finance, and speculation. Mill after mill had to close or work short time, seeing that after having worked double tides in order to take advantage of high prices and a good market, the manufacturers now found themselves face to face with a shrinkage in the prices of manufactured goods of 15 to 20 per cent. below what it had cost them to produce the goods. Nor was there any prospect of immediate improvement, inasmuch that, owing to the falling off of the demand for cotton for the English mills, the price of the raw material seemed likely to fall farther rather than to rise. Miners of all sorts were likewise hard put to it to live; and, most monstrous irony of all, the finest harvest ever known in the United States, unfortunately, fell in with one of the best harvests ever garnered in Europe. Wheat was consequently unsaleable, and hundreds of millions of bushels were wasted; while men who badly wanted them were discharged from work. In every branch of industry similar phenomena were to be observed. America had the honour of commencing the worst crisis of the century.

It was no long time before England felt the effects of the American crisis, though in this country, as on the other side of the Atlantic, men of business, who ought to have been specially capable of forecasting the course of events, imagined that the difficulties would be trifling, that only American business would be seriously influenced, and this only for a time. While everyone prophesied smooth things, the conditions which rendered a storm inevitable had been prepared. The tremendous fall in American securities, and the shrinkage in the price of commodities all round, seem nowadays quite sufficient to have warned the whole mercantile and financial community that the abnormal extension of industrial enterprise had been carried far beyond the point of safety, and that, in particular, the export trade had been pushed far in excess of what could be immediately absorbed. Similar causes had been at work in England, also, to those which occasioned the collapse in America. Though the mileage of English railways constructed had been small in comparison with those built in the United States, the amount of capital sunk had been much greater, and, unlike that invested in America, had not been borrowed from abroad. In addition, the great gold supply from California and Australia had engendered a feeling of over-confidence, based on the gold itself as capital.

Further, though the English banks were sound in comparison with the American, the conclusion of peace after the Crimean War had brought about, on a smaller scale, similar results to those which were noted after the peace of 1815. The war had been a good customer for trade. The money borrowed, and the taxes levied, had been spent unproductively, it is true, but not more so than if they had been thrown away in commanding the production of luxuries for the rich. On the other hand, the war had given a great deal of employment to the working-classes in various departments, and had created a demand for commodities which now ceased. At the same time, also, the war with China, and the mutiny in India, upset the

Eastern trade. Looking back, therefore, at all the circumstances as they are baldly set forth in the chronicles of the time, the wonder seems to be not that the crisis of 1857 proved so disastrous, by reason of the blunders which were made and the want of foresight displayed, but that it did not result in a still more widespread calamity. The record of the imports into New York alone show the lengths to which over-trading from Europe had been carried.

The crisis began in America in August. A little more than two months later, the Liverpool City Bank closed its doors, and then the crash began in earnest in England. Houses connected with the American trade began to fall one after the other in the early days of November. On the 9th of November, 1857 – the date is even still too well remembered in Scotland – the Western Bank of Scotland, with a paid-up share capital of £1,500,000, and deposits to the extent of £5,000,000, suspended payment, and with it fell its ninety-eight branch banks. Then ensued a panic of the same nature as had been seen in New York, but affecting the whole population. The savings not only of the well-to-do of the trading and shopkeeping classes, but of the small farmers and workers in all parts of Scotland, had been placed on deposit in these branch banks. Such deposits were transmitted in great part to Glasgow, to be lent on bills and securities. No sooner did the alarm commence than the local depositors in the Western Bank and other banks began to demand the immediate repayment of their deposits. It was out of the power of the bank, though its shareholders were among the richest people in Scotland and the liability was unlimited, to meet this sudden rush; the directors could not get the assistance they asked for, and down came the bank, to the utter ruin of many at the moment, and to the serious injury of the whole country for a long time.

On the occurrence of a succession of bankruptcies; the Bank of England found itself exposed to a drain of its gold to

Scotland, Ireland, and America, which rushed its rate of discount up in hot haste from 6 per cent. on the 8th of October to 8 per cent. on the 19th, to 9 per cent. on the 5th of November, 10 per cent. on the 10th, and 12 per cent. on the 18th. On the 11th of November the banking department was reduced to £1,462,153, and its securities held against advances amounted to £26,113,453. On the 18th its reserve fund stood at £1,552,686, and the securities at over £30,000,000. The universal panic which set in at this juncture it is needless to describe. All the now familiar features were reproduced on a larger scale than ever. Money seemed likely to become unattainable at any price, and ruin stared even wealthy firms in the face. It is said that the great firm of Overend, Gurney, & Co., of whom more will be heard later on, threatened failure on their own part unless some steps were at once taken to give them immediate accommodation. Such a failure at such a time would have involved ruin to so many, and would have brought about such widespread terror, that the Governor and Directors prayed the Government to suspend the Bank Act of 1844, and permit the issue of bank-notes in excess of the amount of bullion to support them. This was permitted on the evening of November 12th on condition that the bank rate was maintained at 10 per cent. An over-issue of £1,000,000 followed, and in spite of all gloomy forecasts, the financial situation at once began to improve. Thus, for the second time since its enactment thirteen years before, had the Bank Act of 1844 to be suspended, and Government securities to be transferred from the banking to the issue department of the Bank of England, in order to forestall a total collapse of credit.

But the great crisis of 1857 still lingers in the memory of those who lived through it. The numerous houses which failed just before the suspension of the Bank Act, felt that in some way they had been very hardly treated; while those which survived had, like the greatest of all, undergone a shake that seriously imperilled and in some cases eventually wrecked them. Such is

72

the insecurity of this system of production based upon the constant antagonism between gold and commodities, this system of credit based upon anticipation of profits, this system of banking based on lending deposits made at a low rate of interest at a higher rate of interest. And such is the futility of attempting to reconcile the antagonism which lies still deeper in this our modern society, and of which all the rest is but an excrescence, by tinkering with a Bank Act. Palliatives of such a system there may be, but remedy without complete transformation there is none. So long as companies carry out great public works for private profit, and the necessary goods for society are produced solely for individual gain, so long will such ups and downs periodically recur.

Again for the fourth time in the century was the incapacity of the capitalist class to handle the growing powers of man over Nature to the advantage of society clearly exhibited. For the failure of banks and mercantile houses involved the discharge and starvation of workpeople, who for the fourth time in about forty years witnessed the very wealth which they created rise up before them as a monster, dooming them to wretchedness for a time at any rate. In Staffordshire the failure of a bank stopped work in the potteries, and threw 30,000 workers out. In Northumberland the failure of another bank brought collieries and iron-works to a standstill. "The mischief by no means stopped short at the handful of speculators and merchants at the great trading and shipping ports, but extended to the manufacturers whose establishments were brought to a standstill for lack of orders, while the value of their warehoused goods constantly diminished – extended to the carrying trade, since the foreign trade was in utter stagnation – extended to thousands of workers who were thrown out of work – extended even to the shopkeepers whose business was curtailed owing to the greater thriftiness of their customers." In short anarchy had full swing in our industrial order, and the organisers of industry threw the whole business machine out of gear.

"In the cotton factories the depreciation could not be put at less than £500,000, and in the woollen and silk manufactures, on account of the costly nature of their machines, it can be reckoned at no smaller amount. The last factory reports of April, 1850, gave the total of persons employed in the cotton mills at 370,000, and in October, 1857, in consequence of the increased production, the number may be taken at 390,000, who received an average weekly wage of 10s. 6d. per head. During the last three months of the year 1857, the working-hours throughout this entire district did not exceed 36 hours a week, which involved a loss of £1,064,000 in wages, to which must be added close on £500,000 lost through the decrease in the iron trade, in the consumption of coal, oil, and other materials, as well as what was lost by the stagnation in the retail trade. The loss to the woollen and silk workers was probably still greater, since, although this industry employed fewer hands, far more hands employed were deprived of the means of earning their bread. The condition of the iron districts was no better. The Staffordshire Advertiser published a list of 69 blast furnaces which ordinarily gave employment to 28,000 persons in these districts. On the 31st of December they were all out of work. On the same day there were 41 blast furnaces blown out in Scotland, and 16,000 workmen discharged. In South Wales, where the mining industry was carried on as actively as in the above-named districts, a third of the blast furnaces were shut door, wages were reduced 20 per cent., and numerous strikes of the miners took place; while the closing of works in Yorkshire and Durham diminished the wages paid in these counties by £5000 a week. Local newspapers in every part of the country present the same picture. In Birmingham orders were so scarce that the workmen were not employed more than two or three days in the week. In one region the employers discharged part of their workers, in another short time, that is a few days a week, was worked. Public meetings of workers were held to

74

devise means for alleviating the distress, soup kitchens were set on foot, the people were set to work on the public roads, and a vast mass of folk were relieved outside the work-houses. The Poor Law Reports show a significant increase of the poor relieved." (Max Wirth.)

It was the same story everywhere. Even the heavy fall in prices could not tempt buyers, though between the beginning of September and the beginning of December Scotch pig-iron fell from 84s. to 48s. a ton, tin from £140 to £114 a ton, cotton twist 18 to 24 per cent., silk 31 per cent., cotton 33 per cent., hides 30 to 37 per cent., wool 16 per cent., sugar 20 to 28 per cent., coffee 16 to 23 per cent., tea 16 per cent. The exports fell off in the months of November and December £5,000,000. At the same time the fall in nearly all sorts of securities was phenomenal. Yet gold was still coming from California and Australia in constantly increasing quantities; the import of gold into England alone from these two countries being upwards of £22,500,000 in this very year 1857. Needless to add that the power of production and distribution, owing to the great and continuous improvement in machinery and means of transport, was even greater than it had been during the years of the highest prosperity. The liquidation of course showed that credit had been carried to a monstrous excess, and that firms with a capital of £10,000 failed with actual liabilities of ten and twenty times that amount. But the question remains to this day unanswered by the orthodox economists and their successors: Why this inflation yesterday? Why this stagnation to-day? Why this excess of exports last year? Why this diminution this? Why are the workers in full employment this week? Why are they workless and hopeless the next?

That the answers should never have been correctly given by them is the more surprising, since the crisis of 1857 affected far more seriously and obviously than either of the preceding crises every country in the civilised world. Thus France, which by the revolution of 1848 had given an impulse to political agitation and social discontent throughout Europe, in the intervening nine years, entered into the whirlpool of international capitalism and credit to an extent which she never had before. Marx's predictions in his masterly pamphlet entitled "XVIII Brumaire" were fulfilled to the letter. The French bourgeoisie had triumphed, first in the establishment by wholesale bloodshed of the middle-class republic, and then in the establishment of the empire by the cold-blooded massacre of December 2nd, 1851. The stagnation and distrust which had set in with the year 1848 and had since continued now gave place to complete restoration of confidence and credit among the classes in possession. The rate of discount fell, the interest on State loans was reduced, and everything was made ready for that great development of industries, railways, banks, credit establishments and general speculation which completely changed the general character of French business.

Hitherto the French people, the great majority of whom were hard-working, stingy, frugal agriculturists, had conducted their affairs with the greatest caution and prudence. Speculation had been restricted within the narrowest bounds. The object of the Imperial coterie, as well as of the men of business immediately interested, was to change this. To give the workers plenty of work, and the middle-class plenty of business and profit, was the best way to bring about forgetfulness of the past and to establish confidence for the future. The Bank of France, an institution of the soundest character, managed under State control on the most cautious and conservative lines, was soon surrounded by institutions of a very different character, and that influence of the corrupt and greedy German Jews, whom M. Drumont and others have of late so bitterly, but not unjustly, denounced, was firmly established in Paris under the special patronage of the Emperor's most intimate associates, Morny and Persigny. In view of what has occurred since 1870, the rascalities of the Emperor's *entourage* seem less abominable,

76

comparatively, than they did at the time; and, at any rate, they were, like other financial rogueries, a mere embroidery upon the main substance of capitalistic chicane. Such institutions as the Crédit Mobilier and the Crédit Foncier had powers far exceeding those of any ordinary bank or credit establishment. They necessarily were the outcome of an expansion of the system of loans and credit, and themselves pushed to an extreme the tendency of which they were the result.

The idea at the time was that they were in nowise subject to the influence of political or financial crises as even the Bank of France necessarily was, and they started off on their career of fostering the industries and increasing the development of France with an amount of success which justified their foundation. Their means for carrying out their operations of founding industrial undertakings, of selling and buying all sorts of enterprises and their shares by the issue of their own shares, and for conducting banking business of every description, were the paid-up capital of £2,400,000, the issue of bonds, and their deposits and current accounts. This Crédit Mobilier paid 10 per cent. the first year, 1853; 13 per cent. in 1854; 47 per cent. in 1855; 24 per cent. in 1856 – and then came the crash. During the interval vast sums were invested in France in railways, and numbers of great industrial companies were formed to carry out every sort of business, and that rebuilding of Paris was begun which entirely changed the appearance of the city at the cost of millions sterling. On French railways £20,000,000 were spent in 1855 and £21,000,000 in 1856. For France, like England, suffered comparatively little from the Crimean War, to all appearance, while it lasted. Over 1,100 miles of railroad had been built, and in addition to the war loans and expenditure on the development of home industry, millions sterling had been lent to foreigners. When, therefore, the crash came in England, France followed on the same line, and Paris and the other great French cities felt that stagnation of trade, that discharge of workmen, that general glut of commodities which had already manifested themselves in England and the United States.

But precisely the same phenomena were exhibited in Germany, in Prussia, in Austria, in Belgium, in Italy, and even in Scandinavia. No country escaped from this new form of epidemic. For in each and all, according to their degrees, the development of industry had favoured the growth of banks and credit establishments, and again the foundation and growth of these credit establishments had unduly enhanced production viewed from the standpoint of profit-making. The shrinkage of prices which now occurred in one market was felt in all. Manufacturers who had been turning out goods on one level of values had suddenly to accommodate themselves to another and lower scale. The crisis was only more noteworthy in Hamburg than in other German cities, because Hamburg, like Liverpool, was more closely connected with the American trade. The silver mining countries were no more exempt from the consequences of the universal overtrading and undue development of credit than were those which had a gold standard. From Europe the effects of the crisis spread even to Asia. India, and China, as well as the Australian colonies, and South America, underwent a period of bad trade by reason of the disturbance at the centre of the commercial system of the world.

In all the European countries and in America the same results were observable. Republic, constitutional monarchy, or despotism, all suffered alike. Forms of government, banking systems, silver or gold standard were equally of no avail against the industrial crisis. Lack of currency could not be urged as a reason for dull times, when millions of gold a month were coining forward to be minted. Insufficient facilities of credit could not be claimed as the cause of the mischief, when banks and discount houses were wildly competing for mercantile bills. Deficient transport and means of communication could no longer be pointed to as the manifest occasion of a local glut.

The civilised world could produce more wealth with less labour than ever before, and still society in 1857, as in the three previous decades, had been overmastered by its own productive forces and compelled to go into liquidation for a time.

It is this which lends special significance to the crisis of 1857, that even a superficial analysis of the circumstances leads to the elimination of currency, of banking, of credit merely as credit, of political forms, of lack of agricultural land, of protection or free trade, as the primary cause of crisis. An examination of these various points and their bearing upon industrial crises, their extension, their restriction, their palliation, cannot but be interesting; but the real solution of the difficulty lies none the less in the theories set forth in the introduction to this volume.

VI. The Crisis of 1866

It is no easy matter for a society accustomed to certain definite arrangements, especially when those arrangements deal with such apparently complicated matters as currency, banking, bills of exchange, and the like, to understand how the present system has grown up or upon what it is really based. So natural to-day is it for all the well-to-do classes of this country to deposit their savings in a bank and to have an account there, that they can scarcely believe that in France, with all its civilisation, such a proceeding is even now the exception rather than the rule. Banks, in fact, were not originally established to take deposits, and if they had been they would not have got them. The Italian banks of the Middle Ages were established in order to make loans to the various Governments of the cities; the banks of Northern Europe were all set on foot to maintain an uniform currency with which to pay bills of exchange in good money; receiving the bad and debased coin at its intrinsic value, and, after making certain charges, crediting the merchant who thus transmuted his bad coin into good with the balance in the books of the bank. In the same way banks acted as the transmitters of payments for goods to long distances. Out of these necessities and the conveniences which they engendered, the banking system arose and was maintained. And, so soon as this banking system grew and extended, international trade began to assume its modern aspect; for the goods which were exchanged were estimated for the purpose of such exchange in gold or silver, and thus slowly the wider international price was substituted for the fluctuating price of the local markets.

By degrees, therefore, these banks, whether originating in the ways above-named or as goldsmiths and pawnbrokers, developed into the huge joint-stock shareholders' banks of to-day. Private banks having been entrusted with remittances and bank money, or the money necessary to meet bills of exchange, were next entrusted with plate and funds deposited at call. To lend this would, at first, have been regarded as to the full as dishonest and dangerous as it would be to-day for a banker to borrow on his client's securities. But gradually this, too, came to be a portion of the banker's business in addition to his other businesses: to receive deposits of money for safe custody from his clients, and to lend out, what was learnt by experience to be a safe proportion of such deposits on the open market by discounting mercantile bills for other clients, or by lending upon securities realisable upon the market on arranged terms.

But the extension of the banker's business in this direction tended rapidly to diminish the relative importance of his other business. Receiving money on deposit and lending it out again at a profit became so large a part of the banker's daily business that a banker only considered that he entered fully upon his functions while he was doing this. Business with him is literally an affair of other people's money: his own capital being only a sort of security for the proper conduct of the business, and a reserve in case of a run or of a period of continuous lack of confidence. But as savings greatly increased, and the profits to be gained by receiving them on deposit and lending the deposits out at interest became apparent, competition for them steadily grew. So profitable a branch of banking could not be left entirely in the hands of the old private bankers. Joint-stock banks were formed with great capitals, and, whereas the private bankers paid no interest and demanded that a balance of a stipulated amount should be kept, the new institutions all pay interest on deposits having stated terms of withdrawal – the rate of such interest being governed by the rate of discount exacted by the Bank of England; though they speedily surpassed that institution in the magnitude of their total and soon of even their separate operations, in spite of their having no issue of notes.

At the same time with these great joint-stock banks there grew up a whole series of discount houses and bill-brokers, in addition to the large mercantile and accepting houses whose bills had to be dealt with. It was and is the business of these establishments to deal specially in bills with their own and partly with others' capital, rediscounting the bills at a very small profit with the great joint-stock banks. It is in no sense the business either of the banks or of the discount houses or of the bill-brokers, to foster trade or to develop new enterprises. They, in theory, deal only with the results of improved industrial conditions and the increased trade which springs from them. But in practice, as we have seen, the facilities given in times of inflation and high prices have the effect of enhancing both the one and the other. In some cases, means were found to start new enterprises by these financial firms themselves, and the circle of finance was thus not merely indirectly but directly involved in the risks of promotion; in the same way that many of the American banks and the great French Credit Companies were involved. If certain enterprises of a risky description required to be financed, that is to say, if labour and capital are ordered to be expended on undertakings which might never derive benefit from the community nor the community from them, and if the money to pay the labourers and to furnish the plant is advanced upon the shares of a Company, supplemented by its probably worthless bills, it is clear that when the inevitable crash comes it will take the shape of a financial crisis in the first instance, however clearly the failure is due to industrial causes at bottom. All this is simple enough. But so much stress is laid upon the details and complications of banking and finance that at periods of crisis men habitually talk as if the mischief lay wholly in the financial arrangements, and that the mechanical improvement of these arrangements would put everything right. And these remarks specially apply to the crisis now about to be considered.

The great crash of 1857 was not very speedily recovered

from either in Great Britain or on the Continent; while even the United States, with their illimitable agricultural resources, suffered for some time from the stagnation, depression, and utter lack of confidence which followed upon the more acute stages of the panic. Scarcely, indeed, bad trade begun to resume its upward movements across the Atlantic, than the terrible Civil War, which originated in the slavery still prevalent in the Southern States, broke out. The war entailed terrible sacrifices on both sides, but the North being far richer to start with, and receiving, in spite of the civil struggle, crowds of immigrants each year, was certain to win in the long run. Being also preponderant at sea, the Northern navy was able to prevent the South from getting that support from Europe which might have been obtained from the sale of cotton and other slave-grown products. This inflicted a terrible blow upon Great Britain, where also the effects of the great panic of 1857 had only just worn off when the war begun in 1861; and the commercial treaty with France concluded in the previous year was a trifling make-weight against the depreciation of the raw material for the Lancashire cotton mills. There were, however, to the country at large, compensations in the general circumstances of the time for the calamity which fell so heavily upon the workpeople and manufacturers of Lancashire, nor can it be denied that over-production had produced glut before. For the war itself occasioned a demand for English goods up to a certain point, the Limited Liability Act of 1862 gave a great impulse to new ventures, and a supply of cotton from Egypt and India in that and successive years made amends in some degree for the loss of the superior American staple.

That there was plenty of capital seeking investment at this time was abundantly shown by the enormous sums paid into new companies, and the expenditure in the course of a few years on railways of £70,000,000. The close of the American War in 1865 gave a further impulse to new business, which the development of trade with China, India, and Australia likewise encouraged. The threatenings of war between Prussia and Italy on the one side, against Austria on the other, gave as little ground for uneasiness in Great Britain as the war between France and Austria had given in 1859. For, as at all such periods, a neutral power in the position of England gained both in the demands for the manufactures, and in the extension of her already enormous carrying trade. At this period, too, in the year 1865 that is, the total amount of wealth in Great Britain was put at £6,100,000,000. Of course, a capitalised value of this sort is in many respects purely imaginary, as, for instance, the capital value of land taken at a given number of years' purchase of its rents; but on the same basis the capitalised value in 1814 was but £2,300,000,000, or little more than one-third of the amount, while the population in the meantime had increased only fifty per cent. There was again, therefore, nothing in the extent of wealth creation to justify an anticipation of a crash in 1866, nor was there any great evidence of inflation at the time. Some even go so far as to maintain that the crisis of 1866 was not an industrial crisis at all, and it is true that the ordinary symptoms of crisis were not apparent in the trade returns. But it is quite impossible that the downfall of a single house, however powerful, prepared for beforehand as it had been, could have given such a shake to credit and brought about as it did a stagnation in home trade, had there not been a good deal of foolish investment and wild speculation in the years immediately preceding.

At any rate, when on 10th May the great house of Overend, Gurney & Co. suddenly stopped payment, the panic occasioned throughout Great Britain was to the full as furious and unreasoning for the time, though happily for those who lived through it, not so disastrous in its ultimate effects, as the panic of 1857. The firm had only been converted into a Limited Company the year before, by which process a good deal of new capital was introduced into the business. They were at the time still considered by the world at large to be that which they had certainly been in 1856, if not in 1861 – the most powerful firm, as well as the most active and capably managed firm, in the city of London. They stood next to the Bank of England, and their name and influence extended to all parts of the civilised globe. Yet during the very years when their credit stood thus high, and in part for years before, they were encouraging and embarking in enterprises of a character which were so unsound in themselves, and so dangerous from the class of people connected with them, that the veriest tyro in finance would have instinctively shrunk from them, even if they had not been outside of the special business which it was the function of the firm to carry on.

Let us hear the late Mr. Bagehot on the matter, for, assuredly, he could not be accused of under-estimating the ability of English capitalists: "The partners had great estates which had mostly been made in the business. They still derive an immense income from it. Yet in six years they lost all their own wealth, sold the business to the company, and then lost a large part of the company's capital. And these losses were made in a manner so reckless and so foolish that one would think a child who had lent money in the city of London would have lent it better." Yet it was in the power of these sapient nincompoops to break the Bank of England, to occasion such a desperate panic throughout the country, and to injure the credit of Great Britain abroad to such an extent that positively the Foreign Secretary at the time was impelled to send a circular to all our ambassadors abroad, in order to assure foreigners that the bottom had not fallen out of our island – whose total wealth, according to Mr. Robert Giffen, then amounted, to £6,100,000,000.

What renders the whole thing more mysterious to those who do not look below the surface, and more absurd to those who do, is the fact that the Bank of England had, by common consent, an exceedingly good reserve when Messrs. Overend,

Gurney & Co.'s suspension took place – that reserve being then, as it is to-day, the only real reserve retained by the greatest commercial city to carry on the greatest commercial transactions for the international business of the world. But the transactions of the firm of Overencl, Gurney & Co. were so extensive, bills drawn on them had such universal currency, that nobody knew what might be the end of their breakdown, and consequently, bankers, bill-brokers, merchants, rushed pell-mell to the Bank of England to secure to themselves the means of meeting their acceptances, and carrying on their business. Cash or notes were alone legal tender in discharge of debts, and those who wanted to keep their heads above water, as the tidal wave of general distrust swept on, were compelled, as usual, to obtain advances on the best securities they could get "Ma foi j'ai v4eu," said the man who was asked what he had been doing during the French Revolution. "Ma foi j'ai vecu," might have replied many a man of business who was still carrying on his daily round of duty a few days after that memorable 10th May, 1866.

The Bank of England did its best to check the panic, and advanced £4,000,000 in hot haste on stocks, bills, and any good security. But all to no purpose. The banking department ran down to £3,000,000, and then, for the third time in two-and-twenty years, the Bank Act was suspended, relief was given by degrees, and the panic rapidly subsided.

But those who contend that this was merely a currency crisis overlook what went before, and that which followed after. Overend, Gurney & Co.'s failure brought down with it many smaller firms. One hundred and eighty companies were wound up in a few months. And to take one trade only, the cotton trade, not until 1870 did the factories of Lancashire work on the same scale as they had worked ten years before in 1860; though at the time of the crisis a perceptible improvement had begun. The same phenomena of glut and stagnation were again to be noted, and the consequences to English credit on the Continent have already been spoken of.

It is a singular comment on this Overend & Gurney crisis of 1866 that the partner in the firm who was more than any other responsible for their ruin, but who retired before the firm was converted into a Limited Company, should only just (1891) have died worth £1,000,000 in personal property!

VII. The Crisis of 1873

The time had now arrived when great crises, although they may begin with a sudden panic, have also harmful and enduring effects upon industry which extend over many years, and, in the course of the long series of liquidations which they bring about, spread to every country, touching even those nations that apparently have least direct mercantile connection with the point at which they might chance to originate. With the increasing complexity of international trade and financial relations, alike under Protection and Free Trade, it is clear that stagnation in any one region, or in any particular industry, must make itself felt sooner or later in all others more or less; seeing that, in order to realise profits, exchange, first of commodities for gold and then of gold for other commodities, must go steadily and uninterruptedly forward. Such a country as the United States, with its enormous territory still sparsely peopled and in part wholly unoccupied, with its great variety of climate and unprecedented wealth, alike agricultural and mineral, may endeavour to render itself independent of its neighbours by the imposition of high tariffs. But even in this case the necessity for exporting food and raw material in vast quantities involves its inhabitants more and more in the ups and downs of Europe. Hence the low price of grain at the European centres, due to such a cause as an exceptionally good harvest in India or Russia, has prevented many a Western farmer from re-painting his farmhouse and barns, has thus reduced the demand for paint, and thus, in turn, has lowered the price of lead and caused the shutting down of many of the mines of the Western States. Hence, again, men have been thrown out of work and into distress even in that land of plenty in the best of good seasons. This is but one instance out of many, which is not rendered less sad to those who suffer by the fact that on the return of "good times" prosperity reaches a greater height than ever before.

The crisis of 1873, though it did not begin in the United States, as did the crisis of 1857, was, like that great catastrophe, largely due to the course of development in that country. But, taken in all, it had more various causes, it spread over a wider range and had more disastrous consequences than any of the previous crises. Beginning its career on the Bourse, it successively brought down in sympathy the trade, industry, and eventually the agricultural economy, of the entire West. It commenced first of all in Vienna at the commencement of the month of May, 1873, but the consequences of the crisis endured up to the autumn of 1879, and directly involved the whole of Austria-Hungary, the German Empire, Italy and Switzerland, in the injurious effects of its complications. The crisis broke out with redoubled force in America, and brought the English, Scandinavian, and Russian money-markets as well as the industries of France, specially devoted to the production of luxuries, within its range, though the latter country had been prevented by the misfortunes of the war from indulging in over-speculation. The shocks of the great crash were felt at Belgrade, and Bucharest, at Odessa, Moscow, and Nijni Novgorod, at Alexandria, And in South America.

Here we have the international crisis in its most complete form, and lasting in a more or less injurious shape for upwards of six years, and even then the recovery was shortlived in more than one country. Yet, during the sixteen years from 1857 to 1873, the development of production and trade had again surpassed all anticipations even of the most sanguine. And this experience was not confined to any one or two countries. Exports and imports had more than doubled in the United Kingdom, in the United States, in France, in Austria, and in Belgium. Railways, steam-ships, telegraphic cables were facilitating transport and rapidity of communication in a progressive ratio; improvement in the production of iron and steel was so great as to more than meet the increased demands of modern society; while the almost unnoticed application of machinery to agricultural purposes in United States was working a revolution in the production of food-stuffs, to be compared only with that which had already been brought about in the working up of cotton, wool, etc., at the beginning of century.

The most terrible wars in America and in Europe had been powerless to arrest the advance more than momentarily, and Great Britain actually benefited so much by the war between France and Germany that Mr. Gladstone, shortly afterwards, used his often-repeated phrase about prosperity advancing "by leaps and bounds." It is, indeed, needless to enlarge upon the constantly multiplying power of man to produce wealth. The application of science to wealth-creation is now so direct and immediate that the difficulty of at once adopting new inventions and discoveries arises from the fact that in many branches of industry wages are so low that it is cheaper for the employer to proceed with the old methods than to introduce the new. But even this hindrance has only hindered not checked the advance all along the line; and, as each successive period passes and can be compared with the one before, we see clearly that for every person employed in industry the increased production per hour actually worked has again been multiplied many times.

The war of 1870, with its fearful waste of life and material, and the trade losses it had involved to the two greatest continental powers, occasioned an immediate demand on this powerful economical machinery to fill the gap. Even the tremendous war indemnity, which was intended to crush France, had its effect in stimulating the remarkable rebound of trade which commenced on the conclusion of peace. For France, with a power of recovery wholly unexpected, set to work to pay her vast debt, pile up fresh accumulations, and reorganise her army and navy at one and the same time, with an industry and assiduity which perhaps no other nation in Europe could have rivalled. The Germans on their side used the £200,000,000 of indemnity to replace their material and refill their war chest, but also to pay off the various State debts. This put large amounts of capital at the disposal of private persons who naturally wished to use them to a profit again. It is scarcely too much to say, also, that the moral effects of the astounding victories of the Germans over the French and the reconstitution of the German Empire were such that Germany was filled with a new life, and felt invigorated to an extent never experienced since the wholesale devastations of the Thirty Years' War. Hence followed a rush into new undertakings, a desire to extend and beautify the principal cities, and to complete the railway connections between the various parts of the new Empire, for but a fraction of which enterprises the French indemnity could provide the funds.

Though, however, some of the chief causes of the crisis lay in the German Empire, Vienna, as already stated, was the first city to feel its effects. Throughout Austria-Hungary the five or six years prior to 1873 had been years of the most extraordinary development of companies. Railways, coal mines, iron and steel works, sugar factories, and banks were constructed, organised, and started one after the other. In Vienna, in the year 1869, the total of such enterprises set on foot reached the amount of upwards of £80,000,000, of which more than half was paid up. In Pesth, no fewer than 91 companies, with a gross capital of not less than £27,000,000, were quoted on the Exchange. In short, the Austro-Hungarian Empire was for the first time gripped completely within the circle of international capitalist finance, and the company form of industry supplanted the old methods in every direction. As an example of the apparent prosperity which followed, the output of the great breweries increased in five years from 2,978,464 firkins to 5,433,904. According to official returns, State concessions were granted for the formation of 1005 companies, with a nominal capital of about £300,000,000, most of which were supported by foreign capital, and for their mere foundation not less than £100,000,000 were required according to law. There were thus established 175 banks, 604 industrial undertakings, 34 railway companies, 39 insurance companies, 23 mining companies, 8 shipping companies, and 18 hotel companies. In 1866, the total paid-up capital of the banks amounted to 190 millions of gulden, at the end of 1872 to 508 millions. In the first three months of 1873, 15 new banks were established, with a paid-up capital of 72 millions of gulden. The share capital invested in railways nearly doubled in the same time, while the preference shares nearly trebled. So enormous was the amount of capital subscribed and to be expended, that if all the enterprises had been undertaken and carried on there would not have been nearly enough skilled workmen in the country to complete the works. A similar state of things was to be found in Germany. In the year 1872 there were established in Prussia alone banks, building societies, mining companies, railway companies, iron works, etc. etc., with a capital of £76,000,000, while in the same year the total issues on the European Stock Exchanges reached the vast figure of £500,000,000, following upon similar issues to the still greater amount of over £600,000,000 in 1871, without any estimate of premiums.

In Prussia 259 companies were established in 1871, and 504 in 1872, as against 34 in 1870 and 225 since the beginning of the century. Even in the first six months of 1873, companies and loans were issued in Europe to the amount of fully £300,000,000, though the crash was then close at hand.

These figures, and many more might be given, only express, after all, the truth that the continent of Europe had fully entered upon that period of wholesale capitalistic production and speculation which had already produced such disastrous effects on countries economically more advanced. What made matters even worse was the foundation of all sorts of banking institutions, which had little else than stock-jobbing in view. The real object of banks and companies was quite lost sight of, and men were swept into the whirl of speculation without having any other desire than to gamble and to make money in the lottery of the share market. Mortgage banks and building societies gave an undue impetus to building speculations in the great cities, from which Berlin and Vienna still suffer. These building speculations were indeed among the most unsound and ruinous of all the business of the time. The price of land was run up to a purely fictitious level, and loans were made to cover the sites with houses to an extent which, when the crash came, rendered it impossible to recover even a fraction of the principal. The great object was to run up the houses in good, or what were likely to be good, situations, and put a rental upon them which, in nine cases out of ten, was never realised. To give an adequate account of this building mania in Berlin and Vienna would require a chapter to itself. But similar follies can be seen in London on a smaller proportional scale, and the speculative builder who, working on a small capital, must live continuously from hand to mouth, borrowing at usurious rates to complete jerry-built structures, is well-known here at home.

A very short consideration would have proved to the speculators that no possible increase of population could justify the excessive competition for building land and the inordinate sums spent in erecting houses upon it. But at such times nobody reasons. Each expects that the good times will last until he is able to "get out" at a profit, and what the result may be when a crash does come – that is a matter which can be attended to when it presses, not before. What concerned the gamblers for the moment was that building plots were fetching fully ten times what they were unsaleable at a few years before; that they were able to borrow on their purchases up to the hilt; and that no sooner were the buildings above ground than they could borrow up to the hilt again. And so for the time the building companies made an exceedingly good showing and divided up large sums on paper. During the same period railway contractors and speculators such as Dr. Strousberg, who at this time came to London and took a mansion in Grosvenor Place, made vast fortunes likewise on paper, and also constructed railways so badly that, as was the case with more than one firm of English contractors, they obtained so infamous a name for their fellow-contractors of the same nationality that no English contractor has been allowed to build a line in certain countries since. Adulteration in commodities, jobbing and jerry-building in contracts and house construction, such unfortunately is the rule in days of high prices and prosperity such as these before 1873 appeared to be. The swindling and corruption which accompanied the procuring of the concessions in Austria and Germany formed a fitting preface to the shameful stamping which followed in carrying them out. There was thus quite enough inflation in the German-speaking countries at home to render a crisis inevitable, and to ensure that its effects should be disastrous; but the enormous extent to which Germans of all classes had invested their savings in American railways rendered the crash more calamitous when it came.

Germany and Holland, more far-seeing than England taken as a whole, and better informed perhaps by their emigrants as to the prospects of eventual victory, had steadily backed the North during the Civil War, and had continuously purchased American securities at low prices during the whole of the struggle. When the fight was over they reaped their reward, and their successful investments in United States bonds encouraged them to take up those American railway securities with which Europe was now flooded. The development of railways in the United States had attained a height quite unparalleled in Europe, rapidly as railways had been constructed in Great Britain and elsewhere to meet the necessities of increasing trade. In America railways were really

95

the only permanent roads over vast stretches of territory, and it was by this means alone that the great cities could be connected together and the magnificent far West opened up to colonisation. The United States had therefore, even in 1870, seven times the mileage of railway per inhabitant to that which was formed by Europe; and in 1870 the Great Republic had fully 60,000 miles of railway completed and running between the Canadian State line and the Gulf.

It was a period of marvellous "boom" in West and East alike. The first great trans-continental line to San Francisco had only recently been completed, and the inhabitants of that city and of California generally anticipated that the development of the Pacific Slope would rival or even surpass the older settlements of the Eastern States. The farmers of the West, not as yet crushed down under the weight of mortgages as they too often are to-day, were prospering in every way, and, unprecedented though the expenditure on railways had been, there was every reason to believe that it would fully repay the investors and benefit the entire country. Those who have been in the United States at such times know the sensation of general wellbeing and universal progress which is felt throughout the country. Nowhere is a period of prosperity more suddenly and surely exhibited in the lives of the people. During these years when the losses by the war had been replaced and the whole nation thought itself on the full flow of continuous improvement, everybody was making money and nearly everybody was spending it. Good trade in one quarter made good trade in another. The spread of luxury even in the villages of the far West was something astounding. Never perhaps in the history of the United States had the mass of the people been so well off as during the years from 1869 to 1873.

On railways alone it is estimated that not less than £400,000,000 had been expended since 1867, of which nearly one-half was represented by mortgage bonds. It was these mortgage bonds at low prices, with sometimes an accompanying bonus in the shares of the company, which tempted the European investors to invest in America again, as they realised their profits on the United States loans bought back at high prices by the Americans themselves. All this marvellous well-being for the many and fortune for the few was duly reported to their friends and relatives at home by the ten millions or more Germans who were now settled in the United States. For the Germans had benefited even more than the English or the Irish by the settlement of the great West. Small thrifty farmers or tradesmen at home, they went out to the United States with a little capital, prepared to rough it, and to devote many years of their life to building up a happy home for themselves and a moderate competence for their children.

The great through lines of railway which were being built served for them the same purpose as the great rivers had served before, and thrifty, well-to-do German colonies were to be found pushing on steadily along the routes of the main railways to the new unsettled countries which had not yet been overrun. For the Germans did not as a rule linger round the cities in the same way as the Irish, nor did they meddle much with politics until they had made their reasonable competence, or until their own individual interests were directly affected. But now these men in country-township, town and city alike, were getting rich, not slowly but fast. Their habits of life and expenditure were below the scale adopted by native Americans or English when they are successful, and their savings were proportionately greater. Wonderful accounts, therefore, they sent home of what they were doing, and it is not too much to say that the whole middle-class of Germany and Austria looked to America as to the promised land. Those who went put themselves and their capital, under the Stars and Stripes; those who remained and could do so invested their savings largely in the bonds of those American railways which were to bear their relatives to the regions of plenty. The process went on steadily, and this German exodus contributed even more to the wealth of the United States than the Irish colonisation, of which so much more, in England at any rate, has been heard. The injury which was thus done to Germany herself, and the overwhelming competition to which German and other European agriculture would be subjected by the competition of the products from their own fellow-countrymen, were not at first fully seen, while at the same time the pressure of the Imperial Government drove away across the Atlantic many Germans who could ill afford to spend even their passage money. Meanwhile the American railways, with their enormous land grants from Congress, continued to attract European capital, and among others two great new trans-continental lines, the Northern and the Southern Pacific, were taken in hand.

As usual, the causes of the crash were not observed, nor was its imminence believed in, even by businessmen, until the collapse in prices and the helter-skelter rush to sell had well begun. Yet all the symptoms of crisis were well exhibited in Austria and Germany for some time beforehand. A glance at the list of enterprises launched in those countries in the year 1872 alone is sufficient to show that already speculation and excessive construction of permanent works, and over-production, as it is called, had reached their extreme limit. Prices of commodities, of shares in good enterprises, of land, of houses, had all risen, and wages had gone up in at least an equal ratio, attaining a level, in America more especially, higher than anything ever reached before. At the same time the workers in every country were constantly on strike, and efforts were being made to obtain better conditions of existence and shorter hours of labour, so that the wage-earners might in turn derive some benefit from the enormously increased power to create wealth.

The upward sweep of luxurious living among the well-to-do kept pace with the rest of the development. A visitor to Berlin or Vienna, who had known those cities well before the great changes wrought by the recent extension of capitalism, could not fail to be struck with the spread of luxury and display among the middle and upper classes. The simplicity of German bourgeois life had vanished. Ostentation had displaced elegance, and domestic comfort had given way before vulgar profusion. Nor had the people benefited in the same degree even as in Great Britain. The overcrowding, due to the erection of magnificent palaces where labourers' dwellings had formerly stood, had raised rents for the poor for worse accommodation to an extent that could only be paralleled in London or New York. Wages had not advanced in proportion to the dearness of living, and the right of combination was greatly interfered with.

The whole industrial growth of Austria had so concentrated itself in companies, credit establishments, banks, and similar institutions, represented by shares in the Stock Exchange, which were dealt in and settled for day by day, that the great crisis which began in Vienna on May 10th took at first exclusively the form of a Stock Exchange panic, such as might be, and lately was, brought about at the same centre by a war scare. It was even supposed that this might be the beginning and the end of it. That the prices of shares in such companies had been run up far too high by the declaration of fictitious dividends, by assiduous puffing in the parasite press, and by the usual trickery resorted to to keep stocks above their real value, was freely admitted by some German financiers, not a few of whom regarded the commencement of this, as it proved, overwhelming crisis as only a natural and wholesome shrinkage of the price of shares to reasonable dimensions. They were soon undeceived as to the magnitude of the calamity which had befallen the whole of Central Europe and the countries with which their recent operations had brought them most directly into contact. Even the most important agricultural industries of the country, connected as they were, like the sugar industry, in an increasing degree with factories managed and owned by share companies, were represented by shares on the Vienna and

Berlin Stock Exchanges. And the gambling in all these shares was carried on upon a scale hitherto quite unprecedented on the Continent. Creatures of finance too often to begin with, they soon become mere playthings of the stock operator.

At the end of April the Vienna Bourse was already in the first throes of the panic, and herculean efforts were made to meet the threatened catastrophe, which also, it was hoped, would be in some strange fashion conjured away by the opening of the Exhibition that was arranged for the 1st May. Meetings of banks were held to consider if any steps could be taken to restore confidence, and to stem what was still regarded as a mere fall in stocks. But the evil was too deep-seated to be arrested in this fashion. Nothing less than the temporary unhinging of all Austrian finance, trade, industry, and construction of public works, was inevitable. Accordingly, the now familiar spectacle to be witnessed during every really serious crisis was displayed to the world for the first time on the banks of the Danube, on the 8th and 9th of May, 1873. Panic, chaos, wild despair, hopeless madness, collapse of confidence, complete crash in business – such are the words used by eye-witnesses to describe scenes which, they confess, beggared description.

On the 10th May things were at their worst. Every effort was made to lessen the effects of the crash – a guarantee fund was formed, and on May 13th the National Bank, by a somewhat similar suspension of the law to that which the failures of the Bank of England have accustomed us to in London, was enabled to come in some degree to the rescue, and save the situation. But even then it was thought that the crisis was merely a crisis in stocks and shares, and that the extension to trade and industry could be avoided. But by this time all Austria-Hungary was in the whirl of the crisis, and guarantee funds and committees of assistance had to be set on foot in all the principal towns. By degrees the more acute superficial

100

symptoms of the crisis were subdued by the various remedies employed, but the cure of the disease was slow and the recovery greatly prolonged.

For, of course, this Vienna crisis was essentially an industrial, trade, and, in the widest sense, financial crisis, and it was only one peculiar feature of the case that it should have manifested itself, to begin with, in a Stock Exchange form. An increase in the facilities for discounting bills or lending on securities, an inflation of the currency, might give relief to genuine traders, and prevent a complete stoppage of the necessary exchanges, but all remedies of this kind cannot possibly replace wasted capital, find a market for commodities which have no buyers, or pay interest on repudiated loans. And Austria-Hungary, and then America, and shortly afterwards Germany and Holland, had to face all these difficulties, and slowly to overcome them at the expense of great suffering and poverty. But at first it was thought in England, in America, and in Germany, as it had been in Vienna, that business generally was quite sound, and that little more would be heard of the first serious crisis in Eastern Europe. This, too, although all dealing in fresh American issues stopped suddenly, and there was a great and general fall in all American securities in sympathy.

But similar causes to those which operated in 1857, and to a less degree in 1869, were at work in the United States, and it needed but a slight shock from without to bring on another very serious crisis in that country. The astounding growth of business and the extension of railways in America, accompanied by an ever-increasing prosperity for the whole nation, in the sixteen years from 1857 to 1873, in spite of the heavy loss of life and enormous expenditure during the Civil War, have already been spoken of. It was from this wealthy nation that the next blow was to come which would fall with redoubled force upon the trade and finance and industry of Europe, already most injuriously affected by the Vienna crash, which had spread to other countries and had involved every branch of business. New York at this time was literally swamped with railway securities for which, especially after the outbreak of the Vienna crisis, no outlet could be found in Europe. To such an extent had the overbuilding and rash financing been carried, that the moment one bank failed a succession of bankruptcies became inevitable. The crisis there began with the downfall of a firm which had made heavy advances on the securities of the Missouri, Kansas, and Texas Railroad, followed by the suspension of payments on the part of another firm which had acted in the same capacity towards the Canada Southern. Thereupon came the appointment of a receiver for the New York, Oswego, and Midland Railroad.

Directly afterwards, on September 18th, down came the bank of Jay Cooke & Co., with their branch bank of Jay Cooke, McCulloch & Co. in London, in which latter city, however, they had never attained to a very high position, in spite of the fact that they were the financial agents of the United States Government. Their fall was due to their intimate connection with the Northern Pacific Railway, and the affect of it was both immediate and disastrous; the position which the firm had held in relation to United States loans, and the general financial business of the Government rendering their collapse the more serious from all points of view, especially as they had in hand at this very time the negotiations for the formation of a syndicate to float United States bonds at a lower rate of interest. Concerning the details of the general crash and liquidation which followed, it is unnecessary to say much. Banking house after banking house came down, and the New York Stock Exchange was closed, only opening again on September 30th. But great commercial and distributing houses were also obliged to suspend payments. Not a single industry remained unaffected by the collapse, which, as in Vienna, was at first thought to be purely a Stock Exchange difficulty.

Strangers who were in America, or engaged in American

business at the time, were as much surprised at the sudden and universal sweep of the catastrophe as they had been at the previous extraordinary inflation. Throughout the whole of the United States it seemed as if some great disruption had occurred. There was a glut in every department of trade, almost, it may be said, in every warehouse. Mills, factories, and workshops of every kind were closed in the West, as well as in the East, or worked short time. The almost universal suspension of work on the new railways threw tens of thousands of labourers out of work, while the old railways only made such betterments as were absolutely indispensable. The influence of this upon the iron and steel trades, and upon the iron and coal mining industries, was felt immediately. Thousands of men were unavoidably dismissed in these departments, and from a third to a half of the workpeople in the Eastern States were said to be without employment. The number of actual "tramps" during the winters of 1873 and 1874 was placed as high as 3,000,000 out of a total population of little over 40,000,000. When to these are added the numbers who starved quietly at home, the proportion of workless persons to the entire population seems something prodigious. In New York, Pennsylvania, Ohio, and the New England States, the state of things was quite deplorable.

The condition of the West was little better. All prices were down and yet goods were unsaleable. Cotton, wheat, wool, lead, iron, steel, leather, were all selling from 20 per cent. and more below the prices they had fetched before the crisis. Importers were in the same case as the manufacturers and contractors. Even at the full shrinkage they could not realise on their goods. Wholesale and retail traders were in the same hopeless condition unless they had obtained time from their creditors. The whole country looked as if it were suffering from some huge natural catastrophe. It was nothing short of horrible to go through some of the districts where, but a few months before, all the industries had been in full swing, where the people were in the enjoyment of a good standard of living, anticipating the continuance of employment at high wages, and now to find whole towns full of workers standing idle, and not knowing what to expect next. For, once more, it was not only the mismanagement of the past that was to blame for the fearful condition of workless misery into which the industrious wealth-producers had been plunged, but the mismanagement of the present alike in America and in Austria.

There were the unsaleable goods lying to their damage in the warehouses; there was the machinery rusting and depreciating for want of use; there stood the labourers, eager to work and to produce useful articles, or to complete great highways of communication in return for some of this food and these clothes, etc., which were so cheap that they could not buy them. And yet it passed the wit of man, as exercised in modern society, to bring these two sides of production and consumption together for the benefit of all, by reason of the fact that the wit of man in society today is so bemused by the complications of that society that employers and employed alike still imagine that these periods of collapse are inevitable, and that hard times cannot but come. At any rate, 83 railway companies, with a capital of some £50,000,000, suspended payment, and workmen were discharged in every direction. And as the theory of the well-to-do classes throughout the United States is, that no man need ever be out of work except by his own fault, and that a vagrant is to all intents and purposes a criminal, the way in which the unfortunate workers were treated during this sad time for them, may be imagined. America is a hard place for a poor man during a trade depression.

As usual in all countries after a crash of this sort, instead of looking into the methods of production, and the unregulated maladministration of capital, the rich and their governments began to overhaul the banking system and those currency arrangements which, however defective they may be, cannot, by any possibility, create an industrial crisis, though they may and do intensify one when it comes. The United States had devoted itself since the war to the improvement of its general credit; and the steady repurchase of its bonds had placed the Republic in the first rank of borrowers so far as its State debt was concerned. But it had left its paper money, which bore no interest, to settle itself, this paper money being, practically, an inconvertible currency, and silver only legal tender up to five dollars. But although it may be granted that this currency question had some influence, it must surely be clear even to the most bigoted doctrinaire in currency matters that, assuming that the United States had put matters on so sound a footing that no inconvertible paper had been in circulation at all; that the note issue of the banks had been represented by bullion up to their full value; and that the supply of gold and silver had been unprecedently large; still the expenditure of so much labour and capital on railways, on mines, on the production of commodities, and on the provision of luxuries must have brought about a crisis. Losses had been incurred which some one had to pay for, and goods had been produced to such an extent that, the market for them being what it was, further profit could not be made by producing them on the same scale any longer. Consequently, the individuals and companies who had incurred the losses had to go into liquidation; the traders who had more goods on hand than they could dispose of were compelled to ask for time in which to dispose of them; the employers of labour either could not carry on their contracts or get orders for more goods; and the result of it all, no matter how the currency stood, must still have been as it was, that men and women would be thrown out of work and industry would be involved in a crisis.

In such circumstances it is not in the power of banks or currency manipulators to put matters right. Organisation of labour by the community is needed, and of all countries in the world the United States is most opposed to any interference with the anarchy engendered by the capitalist system. And if such crises as these of 1857 and 1873 could occur in America, with its unlimited territory, its vast resources of every kind, and constant influx of the cream of the European populations, many of the immigrants bringing their own capital, it is manifest that the older communities which do not possess these advantages are likely to suffer still more severely from them as time goes on.

But now it was the turn of Germany and, after her, of France and England, to experience the inconveniences arising from the ups and downs of modern trade. So far the Vienna crisis had only partially affected the principal German Stock Exchanges. The period of inflation continued months after the crash in Vienna had disorganised the whole business of Austria-Hungary. In the first six months of 1873 no fewer than 196 new companies, with a gross capital of £25,000,000, were set on foot in Prussia alone, and even so late as July, August, and September, capital to the amount of nearly £15,000,000 was asked for similar undertakings. There was certainly no taking in of sail or preparation to meet danger in all this. On the contrary, the mania for speculation carried on the inflation up to the very last moment. The crash in Vienna took place early in May: yet in October a number of new companies were launched in North Germany. The inflation was rendered greater and more serious in its effects by the gambling shops, mis-called banks, which were set on foot in every German town of any importance, to aid in fostering the premium hunt that was going on, more particularly in the shares of the rotten and over-capitalised building companies which were now at preposterous prices. The total amount of capital required for various enterprises in Prussia far exceeded the possible savings of the nation.

In the end the crash came here too and produced similar effects to those which had been felt in Austria earlier in the year. One after the other the paper-built schemes tottered and fell.

Thousands of work people were thrown out of work, the crisis continuing at its height for upwards of two months, after which the full extent of the glut and stagnation and the consequent distrust was perceived. In Austria the State was called in to help the sufferers from the social bankruptcy, and though the advances were made, of course, to the middle-class, the workers benefited to some extent: in Prussia and Germany the anti-State view was on the whole taken, and the workers suffered the more. The spread of the crisis to Italy, Sweden, Holland, and other countries, where railway and building speculations had been pushed beyond the bounds of all reason, was, of course, inevitable, and, as each nation received the shock, the general glut and stagnation of trade were more severely felt by the rest. Necessarily, for if the workers cease to produce in one part of the civilised world, there is less demand for the articles which they consume themselves and less demand for the luxuries consumed by their employers. Thus, bad trade tends to develop bad trade, as good trade expands the area of good trade, until such time as the world's business has "touched bottom," and the upward cycle recommences with as little foresight and consideration as before by those who form part of it.

In Great Britain, though the crisis of 1873 could not fail to produce a temporary panic, and early in November the rate of discount at the Bank of England ran up to the crisis point of 9 per cent., and there seemed a probability of a renewal of the scenes of 1866 and 1857, the reserve in the bank remained at a sufficient height to check an actual furious rush. Since 1869, the country had been enjoying such marked prosperity, and precautions had been so widely taken after the warning of 1866, that in proportion to the growing wealth of the country the commitments were not excessive. The speculation had not overstepped the bounds of ordinary capitalist prudence in good times, or, at any rate, the losses in Paraguay, Honduras, San Domingo, and the Argentine Republic were small in comparison with the general wealth of the nation, while the orders to

107

manufacturers which these loans and others to the Australian Colonies, New Zealand, and Canada had occasioned, gave a still further impetus to a period of exceptional good fortune.

Thus, the rush for gold to the Bank of England early in November found Great Britain better prepared, perhaps, than at any other time to meet it, and it is interesting to compare the very trifling fall which took place in Consols in November, 1873, with the wholesale deterioration which took place during the earlier panics. Even the American Government securities, which in the circumstances might have been specially sold, only fell ½ per cent. at the time of the greatest depression. It may indeed be said that Great Britain on the occasion of this, the heaviest crisis which had been felt on the Continent of Europe, and possibly in America, escaped with little more that a sharp financial scare and losses to a class of investors who could well afford to lose. That the results of the crisis were felt when the general shrinkage of prices set in a few years later is probable, for it is impossible to say where such a collapse as that of 1873 comes to an end; but for the time being there was assuredly no such industrial stagnation here, following immediately upon the financial crisis of 1873, as had accompanied the previous crises. It was a foreign crash which incommoded rather than permanently injured British trade and industry. For in 1873, 1874, and 1875, prices rose to a higher point, especially for coal and iron, than had ever yet been reached.

In the winters of 1874 and 1875, such was the demand for coal for all purposes, that household coal in London was bought retail at between 50s. and 60s. a ton, or about three times its ordinary price. Similar absurd prices were obtained for pig-iron, cotton, wool, and all raw materials, the prices thus paid being, of course, fully represented in the cost of the finished articles. This is the period so often referred to by opponents of the working-classes of Great Britain as that in which Englishmen drank themselves out of their indebtedness, and

108

when pitmen are supposed to have given beef-steaks to their bull-dogs, while they drank one another's health in champagne. That these were grotesque misrepresentations of the truth needs no demonstration. But, even assuming the statements to be true, at this very time the yearly savings for investment made by the well-to-do, non-producing classes, were estimated at not less than £200,000,000 a year, and the total capitalised wealth of the country was put by the same authority at £8,500,000,000 as against £6,100,000,000 in 1865, an increase of wealth probably quite unequalled in any old-settled country within so short a space of time.

But the reaction, though it did not come immediately, was not far off. If England, thanks to a long series of good luck, did not participate in the miseries entailed by the great international crisis of 1873 on other countries, the United Kingdom was not destined to escape unscathed for more than a few years from the inevitable consequences of a long course of prosperity. A shrinkage of prices even below the lowest point yet touched followed, and with this shrinkage a reduction of wages in every department of industry, which brought on strike after strike, and a discharge of labourers in every department of trade. There was a fearful stagnation and glut in commerce and industry, and so great was the fall in prices that even men who were in a position to know better attributed the change more to the scarcity of gold brought about by the demonetisation of silver and the adoption of a gold standard in Germany and other countries than to the glut occasioned by the use of improved machinery alike in agriculture and in manufacture. Others raised again the cry of "over-production." As if food could have been over-produced either in America or in Europe when hundreds of thousands, not to say millions, of men and women were miserably underfed, but could not afford to buy wheat or even Indian corn in sufficient quantity; though the price of this necessary of life was lower both actually and relatively than it had ever been known to be in modern times. For America was developing her agricultural resources again upon a stupendous scale, and produced in the year 1878, which was a bad year for English trade, no fewer than 420,000,000 bushels of wheat, and the export of American wheat and other produce had now attained such proportions that English agriculture was crushed by its competition.

The marvellous improvement in transport and cost of freight, which rendered it cheaper to send grain from the far West to London than to send it from the Lothians, had its practical disadvantages for Great Britain in the effects which it produced upon that which is still the greatest industry in this as in other countries. Agriculture in the form of grain-growing became unprofitable in these islands except upon the better soils, and the system of landownership and land cultivation in England does not allow the greatest advantage to be taken even of favourable opportunities. Grain-growing fell off more and more, and the numbers of live stock were materially reduced. Hence, although the workers of the cities found that their wages went further when they were wholly or partially employed, and the well-to-do classes were able to purchase all the articles needed for the supply of their households from 25 to 40 or 50 per cent. cheaper than ever before, yet the working-classes as a whole had little to congratulate themselves upon. Their uncertainty of employment became worse and worse. The agricultural labourers who were unable to get employment on the land, partly owing to the increasing severity of American competition, and partly owing to the introduction of labour-saving machinery into agriculture in this country as elsewhere, crowded into the cities and still further intensified the competition for employment in periods of stagnation by swelling the numbers of those out of work. The same causes were at work at the same time among the small farmers and peasant proprietors of France, Germany, and Austria. There also the machine-sown and machine-reaped grain of America was bringing about the ruin of the agriculturists, and attempts were made to lessen by taxation the damage done to this class by the unprecedented invasion of the European markets by cheap food from America and later from India. The protective duties imposed with this object in view had, of course, the effect of raising the cost of subsistence to the urban population.

Though there was no actual crisis in England or in any other European country between 1873 and the fall of the Union Générale in 1882, the heavy losses on Turkish, Peruvian, American, Egyptian, Paraguayan, and other foreign loans, the fall of the Glasgow City Bank in 1878, and the consequent shock to business and credit, brought about a period of stagnation and shrinkage of prices which lasted with but little improvement for the mass of the people for several years. It will shortly appear, indeed, that we have entered upon an epoch when periods of a long, slow drag of liquidation below the surface, coming in quick succession, have replaced the panic and crash of the earlier crises. That the effect is precisely the same, and the injury to the mass of the people possibly even greater, cannot be doubted. But the crisis of 1873 is so far the last crisis which has taken the old form. Since then the capitalist class has learnt the art of combination and mutual support in times of danger without, however, taking any care to safeguard the interests of the people.

VIII. The Crisis of 1882

THE crisis of 1882 in Paris, which was the crisis of the Union Générale and its tributaries, reads like a financial nightmare, and has formed the basis of Zola's novel, **L'Argent**. It was a clever and a taking notion that the Catholics should establish a great banking and promoting enterprise of their own, supported by the wealth of the rich devotees of Holy Mother Church and the accumulations of the religious bodies, wherewith to meet the ungodly and the scoffer, the Jew, the worldling, the freethinker, and rout them even in the temple of Mammon their god. And the man who, if he did not conceive, at any rate executed this brilliant project with, for a time, amazing success, was, of course, as little troubled with religious prejudices as he was affected by moral scruples. If ever there was an astounding effort in the way of financial balloonery successfully made and its speedy collapse rendered certain from the commencement, this of the Union Générale was that one. It lasted four years, from 1878 to 1882. Had the head of the enterprise been honest, it is possible that the foundation might have been laid for a gigantic business. As it was, these four years witnessed the rise and fall of a gigantic fraud.

If, as some consider, the Union Générale was simply a stock jobbing experiment, it would certainly not be worthy of consideration in these pages. Mere panics in stocks, though interesting to some extent as showing the excitement and the gullibility of men in such matters, and how even sober investors may be drawn into foolish action at times of general elation or general depression, may and do occur from political or other causes without producing any serious effect on the general well-being. But the upset of the Union Générale had a direct influence upon industry and commerce, and, coming at the time it did, had its share in bringing about the long depression which

113

prevailed in Great Britain and other European countries from 1883 to 1888. It may be doubted indeed whether France herself, with all her industry and natural advantages, has yet fully realised the mischief done by the Union Générale and the failure of the Panama Canal. The one beginning by operations in the region of banking and the Stock Exchange, ended by doing much mischief to industry; the other commencing as a legitimate enterprise for the improvement of communications is ending as a cause of serious financial disturbance.

M. Eugene Bontoux, the founder and organiser and destroyer of the Union Générale , was a man of no greater ability or foresight than dozens of others who may be met any day in the vicinity of the great Bourses of Europe. He had neither the powerful intelligence of a Vanderbilt nor the unscrupulous and crafty cunning of a Jay Gould; yet, in a few months, he obtained control of resources from the public which placed him on a level with the magnates of finance and earned for him the immortal honour of having forced a Rothschild to commit suicide.

The causes of his temporary success are not far to seek. First, he began his operations at an exceptionally favourable moment. France, in the amazingly short space of seven years, had, to all appearance, recovered almost wholly from the losses occasioned by her defeat in the great war. She had bought back the greater part of her loans from abroad; had carried out a series of important public works in the shape of railways, canals, docks, warehouses, etc.; was in process of reorganising her army and navy; had escaped the crisis of 1873, which had inflicted such serious damage on Austria, Germany, the United States, and other countries; and had at the same time accumulated savings on a large scale. All this had been done notwithstanding the political intrigues and changes of Government which harassed the Republic, and now France stood ready to take another move forward as an important financial influence in Europe. Secondly, the policy of the statesmen of the Republic had roused Catholic feeling and had encouraged Catholic unity to an extent which they had scarcely reckoned upon. Shut out from the political power to which they considered themselves entitled, Catholics welcomed the suggestion that they should make themselves felt in the sphere of finance, which was under the control of their enemies. Thirdly, the French market offered special opportunities for the successful inauguration of such a scheme as M. Bontoux's, owing to its lack of any proper regulations in regard to company-mongering. A company could buy its own shares on the French Stock Exchange, either before or after they were fully paid-up, and thus create a false scarcity of stock and manipulate a fictitious premium with the shareholders' own money. Then, on the strength of a high price thus artificially established and maintained, the company could make a further issue of shares before the first shares had been fully paid. It was upon this combination of favourable circumstances that the Union Générale was founded by M. Bontoux.

Recent experience in Austria and Germany was, to the misfortune of the public, completely disregarded, and M. Bontoux, though he came forward from his connection with an Austrian railway with none too clean hands, was received as a financial genius by Catholic society in France. The object of the Union Générale, as was boldly proclaimed on the face of the prospectus, was to bring together the capital of good Catholics, and to centralise the financial interest of bishops, religious missions, and private companies. The union started on its eventful career with the prayers and blessings, followed by the deposits, of the faithful. Those deposits rose from less than £1,000,000 at the end of 1878, to upwards of £5,000,000, in 1881. Branches were set on foot in many French cities, and in Austria. And then the gambling began in earnest. The money of the shareholders and depositors was used to buy the shares on the market, thus forcing them up to a preposterous price; and the shares having been divided, they were again run up in the same way.

This, however, was not the worst part of the matter by any means. Gambling on the Stock Exchange, like gambling at Monte Carlo, is a matter of small importance, except to those who waste their time and squander their money. What one loses another gains. But it is a very different thing when the money which people cannot afford to take from useful business is used to employ labour on enterprises which have no chance of succeeding eventually. And this the Union Générale was forced to do, in order to justify the tremendous premium at which its shares were quoted, and which pulled up the whole market with them. Then set in a regular tussle between the "bulls" and the "bears," – the gamblers for the rise and the gamblers for the fall. Among the latter were the Jews, who knew right well that the whole thing was fraudulent; that the investments made and enterprises undertaken were rotten; and that sooner or later a crash was inevitable. Yet such was the infatuation of the Catholics, followed by the general public, that at first the Jews were beaten. In the long run they had their revenge, and in the spring of 1882 the Union Générale fell.

It is the fashion to say that this was simply an affair of the Bourse; but it is clear, from the course which events took afterwards, that though Paris was the chief seat of the inflation, other markets were very closely concerned, and other industrial centres were most seriously affected. From 1883 to 1888 was a time of low prices and general stagnation of trade. It was a long, slow, grinding crisis in Great Britain, which was felt in every trade, and was reflected in the depression of every industry. There seemed to be a permanent glut and over-production. Furnaces were blown out in every iron district; collieries were shut down, or were running at a loss; ships were laid up to such an extent, owing to the falling off of the freights, that shipowners began to fear that our carrying trade was departing from us. All this meant, of course, thousands and tens of thousands of men out of work, a heavy call upon the Trade Unions for the support even of skilled men who could get no employment, to such an extent that even the most powerful of them saw their solvency threatened. Then followed meetings of the unemployed in London and in all parts of Great Britain, applications for the State organisation of labour, the West End rioting, and the Mansion-House Fund, due wholly to the scare occasioned. It was, in fact, a crisis of the most serious kind, none the less dreadful because at the very same time there seemed to be no equivalent shrinkage in returns to income tax, and the ordinary trade of the country was proclaimed by experts to be "sound." The workers suffered for the blunders made by the "captains of industry" and the "organisers of labour."

A careful examination of the period through which we have but just passed exhibits precisely the same features on both sides of the Atlantic that have been manifested in former times of crisis. A great advance in the production of wealth and improvement in the cheapness and rapidity of transport in every department, accompanied by bad trade and stagnation. In the iron industry, the substitution of steel for iron, the extension of the Bessemer process, and the adoption of the Thomas-Gilchrist process, immensely reduced the cost of production. In shipbuilding, an increase in the size and speed of vessels without precedent since the introduction of steamers, and a corresponding reduction in the quantity of coal used to obtain a given rate of speed, materially affected the carrying trade: the length of voyage on all the great sea routes being reduced by from twelve to twenty per cent. in a few years. In textile industries, though no great leap forward could be recorded, the steady rate of progress maintained since the beginning of the. century was kept up, in spite of the fact that the competition in neutral markets, and in India itself, for our cotton goods, rendered the rate of profit on the turnover small in comparison with the huge gains made in the early days when our Lancashire

117

manufacturers had virtually a monopoly of the trade. At the same time the coal mining industry was proceeding along the same path of an ever-increasing output per man employed. In ten years in the iron industry there was an increase of 1,750,000 tons of pig produced and used by the same number of hands. The introduction and improvement of machinery in carpentery, and joinery, and cabinet-making, in stone-cutting, in brick-making – all had the same effect on production, in the way of making commodities cheaper, and the number of hands employed in each department to produce a given amount of useful articles less and less. Now also electricity was beginning to show, especially in the United States, how ingenious and surprising experiments, made a few years before in the laboratory by the unselfish enthusiasm of a Faraday, could be turned to the practical use of mankind. Electric lighting, electric propulsion, electric telegraphs, electric telephones, electric power in chemistry, all became part of the ordinary life of mankind. The older societies could scarcely keep pace with this new development. "Vested interests," and cheap labour combined, have headed back progress even in Great Britain, and many a petty township of the Far West of America is consequently much better furnished with all the new appliances which science had placed at the disposal of the community than the metropolis of the British Empire. Once more, however, it was clearly proved that all the changes, which should have proved so beneficial, in nowise stayed, but on the contrary rather prolonged, the stagnation on both sides of the Atlantic.

It was in the midst of this depression, occasioned again by superfluity of wealth and the excessive power of man, as it would seem, over the forces of Nature, that all sorts of proposals were made to deal with the sad state of things which prevailed for the working-classes of the United Kingdom. The fearful famine in Ireland, largely arising from the drain of wealth to Great Britain to pay absentee rents, naturally produced political and social disturbance of a serious character.

118

In England, where working-people take starvation as a mere detail in their dreary career of pleasureless toil, there was, it is true, a little dissatisfaction expressed; but as nothing seriously disagreeable occurred, the governing classes contented themselves with setting forth the usual series of absurd remedies for evils which can only be met by dealing with their causes at the root. Thus it was but a few years ago – but the fact is already forgotten – that well-meaning people stumped the country in favour of thrift for labourers who were earning not more than twelve shillings a-week all the year round, including their extra pay during harvest. Some, too, held forth on the advantages of temperance as a cure for bad trade. A third party earnestly advocated State-aided emigration. A single tax upon land values, as preached by Mr. Henry George, was the nostrum of a fourth. Others, again, pointed to peasant proprietary as a necessity if a national catastrophe were to be escaped. It was at this time also that the "Bitter Cry of Outcast London" was published, and created a considerable stir. The public was beginning very slowly to recognise the fact that all this stagnation might be owing, not to outside influences, but to arrangements which might be satisfactorily controlled if only they were studied. >From this to action is, however, a very long way.

The main facts of the situation were put on record by me at the time in the **Nineteenth Century** in reply to those who contended that the glut and depression were due to the inability of this country to supply itself with food, and to over-population which could only be met by emigration. "We are now (1884) dependent on foreign sources for half our food supply, which we obtain partly in return for goods exported, and partly in payment of interest on capital lent. To devote more labour to raising food than we could get it for by devoting less labour to producing other commodities is clearly bad policy so long as we command the sea and can carry on such exchange. It is not the amount of food which can be grown in these islands that limits population, or what has been called the supply and demand of labour in Great Britain. That depends upon the state of the world-market for goods and the profit which has been made by the capitalist class under the present conditions of production. Thus there is over-population, and thousands of men are out of work all along the Clyde to-day; but about two years ago there were not hands enough to do the business which flowed into the shipyards, and mere boys not out of their apprenticeship were coming from other centres to earn 32s. a week as rivetters. Is this sort of 'boom' and depression, with its accompanying periods of over-work, followed by slack time and over-population, due merely to the natural increase of our people? Assuredly not. There is some other cause at work to make useful labourers useless within a period of a few months."

"But I deny the actual over-population, so far as the labourers are concerned, altogether. Never, assuredly, was the power of man over nature so great as it is today. Never in the history of the human race was so much wealth raised with so little labour. Relatively, fewer hands are employed in the iron, coal, cotton, wool, and other industries than was the case a few years ago, yet a much greater quantity of wealth is produced. A few figures will make this quite clear. Thus, in the coal industry, 538,829 persons employed in mining and handling coal above and below ground, in the year 1874, extracted 140,713,182 tons of coal. In the year 1883, 514,933 persons produced 163,737,327 tons, an increase of over 23,000,000 tons, though 24,000 fewer persons were employed. In 1874 the miners won 261 tons of coal per head; in 1883, 334 tons a head; yet in the latter year 53,896 of them were out of work – became over-population that is. In the working of iron and steel 360,356 persons were employed in 1872 and produced and used 6,741,929 tons of pig-iron; in 1883, 361,343 persons were so employed, and they produced 8,490,224 tons, or an increase of 1,750,000 tons for virtually the same number employed! In the cotton and flax industry 570,000 persons used 1,266,100,000 pounds of cotton in 1874; while in 1883 but 586,470 persons used 1,510,600,900 pounds. In every case a trifling increase or actual decrease of persons employed, contemporaneously with a great increase in production. All this while population has been increasing at the rate of 10 per cent. in every ten years; so that the numbers of actual workers remain stationary, or decrease, while the whole population increases. The overpopulation then arises not from a decrease in the powers of production but from their increase. Improved machinery gives greater wealth to the employing class, but renders employment for the workers more uncertain, substituting in many departments women's and children's low-priced labour for that of men, and brings about the periods of universal crisis, such as that we are now suffering from – over-production, over-population and the rest of it – more often and renders them more severe. .... Mr. Mundella assures us triumphantly that the returns to income-tax have increased from £578,000,000 to £601,000,000 during even these years of depression."

I have made these extracts even at. the risk of repetition, because the figures were brought together in the midst of the stagnation, and it is worth while to recall them now. Out of the population of 26,000,000 in England and Wales at that date, 16,500,000 belonged to the non-producing sections.

In the admirable analysis of the statistics of the United States between the years 1870 and 1880, made by my able correspondent, Dr. H. Stiebeling of New York, in his pamphlet, **Das Werth-Gesetz and die Profit-Rate**, the truth appears far more clearly than we in England, with our very imperfect statistical department, can as yet exhibit it. Thus, in 1870, the total capital embarked in the factory industry and in production by hand in the United States amounted to 2,780,665,969 dollars, or, putting roughly 5 dollars (instead of 4.85 dollars) to the pound, £556,000,000. The amount paid in wages in the same year was 620,467,474 dollars or, say, £125,000,000; and the total product amounted to 3,385,860,383 dollars or £677,170,000. The number of the workers employed was 2,052,996; the horse-power represented 2,346,142 horses; and the number of factories and workshops amounted to 252,148, representing 11,027 dollars or £2,205 as the capital of each establishment.

Thus, in 1870, 2,053,996 labourers produced a total value of £677,170,000 or £300 a head, receiving in wages 620,467,474 dollars or £125,000,000, representing £60 a head, the profit being 529,045,688 dollars or £106,000,000.

In 1880, however, the total capital in these same industries had increased to £925,000,000 and the total paid in wages to £190,000,000. The entire product had increased to a value of £1,074,000,000, the number of the workers employed to 2,732,595, and the horse-power to 3,410,837. There were in 1880, however, no more than 253,852 establishments with a capital of £3,600 each, and every worker produced 1798 dollars or £360 in the year, of which he obtained nearly £70 in wages.

Thus, in this decade, the productive power of these American industries had increased 58 per cent., while the number of the workers had increased only 33 per cent., and the number of establishments had increased inappreciably in proportion to the capital employed. Therefore it is manifest that in America, as in Great Britain, as the official statistics prove, the power of production is increasing in a far higher degree than the increase in the number of the workers employed. Consequently, what is defective in the existing system of manufacturing commodities is the co-ordination of the two parts, the living and the dead productive forces. In this very period, 1870 to 1880, the United States passed through a serious crisis with its following years of stagnation and depression, proving once more that the wealth of the country for the well-to-do may be growing, even while the workers are in many branches of trade out of work and starving.

How soon the exhibition of the truth may induce all classes to endeavour to comprehend the facts and to solve the problem either in co-operation or in conflict depends upon the occurrence of economical developments, of which none can foresee exactly the times and seasons.

IX. The Crisis of 1890

With the rising cycle of trade which began at the end of 1887 or the commencement of 1888 we approach the last crisis of the century. The long periods of low prices, accompanied in Great Britain as well as in other countries by a low rate of discount, was felt to be coming to an end, when it was observed that the stocks of raw material and metals had run down to so low a point that even the slightest additional demand would bring about a rise of prices. The old adage that "John Bull can stand almost anything but he can't stand 2 per cent.," had certainly not been borne out during the five years. He had stood a low rate of discount without rushing into any new or doubtful enterprises on a large scale. That a vast deal of business had been done in spite of the bad times, at a profit to somebody, was proved conclusively by the dividends which were paid on the shares of all the good banks in London and the country, as well as by the steady rise in income-tax returns under the head of profits on trade, etc. This was the more surprising, inasmuch that agriculture as a profitable industry was going from bad to worse all the time, and the numbers employed in agriculture, which had fallen from 2,000,000 in 1861 to 1,400,000 in 1881, were still further declining. Moreover, the prices of all commodities being so very low, this income represented a purchasing power of certainly more than 15 per cent. above that which it would have represented in the previous decade, thus affording the comfortable classes a larger margin for saving than they could have relied upon having when prices were higher and trade brisker. No greater proof could be afforded of the elasticity of the capitalist system for those who are already well-to-do than the figures of income and profits for the income-receiving class in Great Britain and Ireland during that period from 1883 to 1887; when every industry was depressed so far as the amount realised for commodities was concerned; when, as has been seen, many thousands of workers were out of employment, and Ireland was suffering from famine. For investment of savings was going on in the Colonies, in India, and in South America, as well as in the United States and elsewhere, upon a scale which would have denoted a high point of prosperity in any other country. But the savings of the United Kingdom in an ordinary year being estimated at £200,000,000, out of a total gross income of £1,300,000,000, any less investment in the year betokened accumulation. When, therefore, the tide began to turn, the rush was likely to be very vigorous.

The special feature of this period of inflation, which lasted for nearly three years prior to the crash of 1890, was the establishment of trusts, and combinations, and "corners," and promotion companies, on similar lines to those adopted in America. The word "trust," however, has not the same signification on both sides of the Atlantic, nor does it always mean the same sort of organisation either in the United States or in England. Trusts in England are for the most part nominally investment companies, which assume to be able to average an investor's risks better than he can do so for himself. Really, they are either companies specially created to dispose of the unmarketable securities which financiers in the city are unable to induce the public to purchase in any other way; or they are mere agencies for the promotion of other companies, which the actual promoters do not wish for any reason to figure in under their own names. There are exceptions, of course, but the majority of the trusts which have grown up in the city of London during the last few years come under one or other of these heads. Seeing that, as a rule, these trusts do not publish full lists of the securities in which they invest, it is possible for all sorts of petty frauds to be committed, and for money received to be utterly thrown away upon worthless enterprises, and still that the public at large should imagine that the directors are doing a most respectable and responsible business.

Another and more important change in regard to the city of London is the ever-increasing preponderance of the great joint-stock banks in comparison with the Bank of England. Such banks as the London and Westminster, the National Provincial, the London Joint-Stock, and many more, with their millions of deposits and their enormous business have become practically supreme in the ordinary daily affairs of London. At the same time, the whole of their ultimate reserve to meet troubled times still lies at the Bank of England, and that reserve has lately been considered insufficient and dangerous. Whether it is insufficient or not will probably never be tested until a complete crash does come. People in the city are exceedingly conservative, and slow to meet changing conditions. Their regular business does not encourage the exercise of foresight to any great extent, Indeed, it is commonly said that a man who attempts to see farther than the currency of a three months' bill is certain to lose his money. What each has to do is to make the best of the circumstances immediately around him, and as one of those circumstances is that the Bank of England should hold for the joint-stock banks an absurdly small reserve in proportion to an enormous business, the general tone about that as about other matters is, "Well, it will last my time."

To those who are not so experienced in business, the mere theorists who regard the matter from without, it does seem somewhat ridiculous that the rate of discount at the Bank of England, which guides the rate for bills in actual daily business and not merely for advances on securities, should be moved up and down like mercury in a tube, because a few hundred thousands or millions worth of gold goes into or is taken out of the bank coffers. Still more ridiculous to the lay mind do these fluctuations appear to be when the total trade of the country is taken into consideration, and the fact that the gold withdrawn or deposited forms but a small fraction of one day's operations at the Clearing House. The general uncertainty and doubt due to such a state of things it is needless to enlarge upon. Twenty years ago an able and cool writer, who was certainly no alarmist, pointed out the increasing danger of the situation. Though twenty years have passed, Mr. Bagehot's fears have not been realised, and it is natural to suppose that what has been avoided in the past will be avoided in the future. But if, as seems certain, the whole capitalist system is about to undergo a crucial transformation, it would be well that as the State (which always has come to the aid of the Bank of England in critical times, and will certainly come to its aid in times still more critical), is directly interested in bringing about a peaceable and orderly change, a careful examination should be made of the position from the point of view of the entire community as well as from that of the banking and business world.

For banking is by no means the only department of our present system in which changes of kind as well as of degree are going on. While private banks are being, all of them, forced to combine to a greater or less extent, and to form limited companies, private business firms are being more and more driven in the same direction. But this extension of the company form of industrial enterprise, quite does away with any personal relation between employed and employer, and, besides that, not unfrequently turns the business from a national into an international concern. The company form of industrial enterprise, that is to say, beginning with water-works, canals, railways, cable lines, and other undertakings, which required far more capital than any single individual or firm could command, has now absorbed, or is in process of absorbing businesses which seemed to depend for their success upon the zeal and capacity of the individual heads of the house, and upon the reputation which the firm's name carried with it in the home and foreign markets. Now, the name is retained by the company, and the partners form, for a time at any rate, a portion of the Board of Direction; but the main responsibility rests, as in the case of a

128

great railway or a great bank, on the manager, or managing director, who receives a large salary for his services, and may or may not be a large shareholder.

The shareholders, of course, have no real control over the business. Their function is confined to holding their shares with satisfaction when they receive good dividends and their shares – theirs today, somebody else's to-morrow – are quoted at a high price; with grumbling when dividends fall off, and their shares are reduced in saleable value. Every company of this sort which is formed extends the area of Stock Exchange transactions and introduces the element of mere gambling into purely industrial business. A company has no responsibility in a moral sense, and the old idea of the individual sagacity of the farseeing employer, who, being the fittest, survived in the furious competition of the market, manifestly cannot be held to apply to huge establishments with a vast number of shareholders; the largest owners being, perhaps, men and women who never were within two hundred miles or more of the property which by legal convention they own. The theoretical and practical effect of all this development of companies will be seen in the sequel.

Banks, mercantile and shipping companies, and great credit establishments, have long been, by the very nature of their business, international to a greater or less degree. But the development of industrial companies having branches of their industry in different countries is comparatively recent. Now, however, it is by no means unusual for great English industrial companies to have factories and workshops and mills and shipyards, created by English capital and owned by English shareholders, in foreign countries. Thus, Armstrong, Mitchell & Co. have works in Italy; Palmer & Co. have works in Spain; Cammells & Co. have works in Russia and, I believe, in America; Coats & Co. have mills in America for sewing cotton, and so on and so on; while, on the other hand, foreign sewing-machine, and type-writing, and watch companies establish branches for production as well as for distribution here. All this shows how the national form of production, notwithstanding all tariff regulations, is giving way slowly to the international form, capital being, of course, utterly indifferent to any considerations of patriotism or morality, profit being its sole end.

In the same way all raw materials, metals, etc., being now bought and sold by reference to the price ruling in the world-market, it is quite impossible for any group of men who may be desirous of making a successful combination to purchase and hold all the stocks of any article, whose price they think to raise by reducing the temporarily available supply, unless they take full account of the production in all parts of the globe. This is particularly the case with respect to articles of small bulk and weight in proportion to their average price. Now, when the shrinkage of prices had continued so long that, owing to increased demand and reduction of supply, the stocks had been brought below the level which the probable demand in the near future seemed to require for its satisfaction, it was certain that a rise of price would follow. Of all the metals in use, copper had fallen perhaps as heavily as any, except pig-iron, in relation to the price in gold which rules the market of the world. So heavy had been the fall in the prices of all metals since the decade 1871 to 1881, that all sorts of arguments were made to show that it was the scarcity of gold and not the increased power of production which had brought about the shrinkage. But now a recovery seemed possible, and a plan was formulated in Paris to make a "corner" in copper after the pattern of the monopoly in petroleum established by the Standard Oil Company in the United States, and similar monopolies, which had been very successful for those who projected them and carried them out.

The fact that such a scheme should be entertained, and its realisation attempted by powerful groups, showed that, in the opinion of the shrewdest calculators, the time was at hand for another "boom." They, therefore, set to work in Paris to obtain control of the supply of copper in sight, and to limit the production by purchasing a limited product from certain great mines at a good price, on condition that only a certain amount should be produced. They fixed their price at £70 a ton, the price of copper when operations commenced being a little over £40 a ton. That the whole copper industry should be deranged by this action affected, of course, the speculators not at all. But they had miscalculated the market themselves. Without going into the details minutely, it is sufficient to say that had they fixed the price at £55, or possibly even £60 a ton, they might have succeeded in carrying out their plan to their own profit. The Chilian mines, for instance, cannot be profitably worked when copper falls below £55 a ton. But £70 a ton was not only a price sufficient to induce the opening of these and other mines, but it was a price high enough to persuade holders of copper in various forms to melt it down, and to supply its place with a cheaper metal wherever possible. So, within a very short time, it was discovered that, in order to keep up a price permanently so much in excess of the permanent cost of production as £70, it would be necessary to buy up all the copper mines on the planet, shut down fully half of them altogether, and limit the product of the remainder. Thereupon, down came the whole edifice, and one of the most important of the French credit establishments – the Comptoir d'Escompte – proved to have been so deeply involved that it was practically ruined, though bolstered up and set going again in another shape after the suicide of the man most responsible for its collapse.

The Salt Union, which was subscribed many times over, is an instance of a similar attempt to limit competition and permanently raise the price of a commodity, this time of a necessary of life to the consumer, by a convention between the producers. At the time when this combination was launched, the parties to it, producers and promoters alike, were for the most part in a very bad way. The producers had been steadily losing money, owing to the low prices, for many years, and some of them were under absolute threat of sale from the bankers to whom they owed money. The Union was organised and brought out successfully, the wholesale price of salt was forced up without, of course, the slightest increase of wages, and the manufacturers who were wise enough to sell their shares in time cleared themselves of their liabilities, while the public had the privilege of paying about £9 a ton retail for salt, which it costs about 6s. a ton to produce. The wholesale price has now fallen prodigiously, and the whole Union seems likely to follow the course of the "corner" in copper; though probably the public will long continue to pay the inflated prices for small quantities for the benefit of the middleman.

These two instances and the constant endeavours made to form "pools" in the iron and other industries, show that capitalists are beginning to try to limit that competition which they have hitherto upheld as beneficial, in the same way that competing banks agree upon a common rate of interest, and railways upon a common rate of transport to the same terminus.

To return to the main events prior to the great crisis of 1890. Throughout the years 1888 and 1889 and the early part of 1890, there was a general recovery in every department of trade. American breweries and industrial enterprises, Argentine loans and railway concessions, Mexican railways and mines, United States railway issues, Colonial loans, were all floated off with ease, in addition to the large number of English breweries and industrial businesses which were turned into companies and occasioned transfers of capital during the same period. Promoters, stock-brokers, contractors, engineers; lawyers, and printers were all doing a splendid business, and the successful issues resulted in an increase of orders to factories and works which were already busier than they had been for years before. As business improved freights began to rise, and the idle tonnage was absorbed, until instead of the Thames and the Tyne, the Clyde, the Mersey, the Humber, and the Tees being blocked with vessels for which no employment could be found, everything in the shape of a steamer that could pound along at nine or ten knots an hour was chartered, and orders were being given in every ship-yard for larger and still speedier vessels to deal with the growing trade. Good times had come once more, and once more that same working population which it had been proposed to ship off to the Colonies as mere human surplusage was absorbed into the capitalist workshops and was even working overtime. The comparison in this respect between 1886 or 1887 and 1889 ought alone to be sufficient to convince the least observant of the absurdity of the current theories as to the causes of "over-population" and "bad times" for the mass of the people. The improvement was felt in every direction, and among other symptoms of well-being was the reduction of taxation and a lowering of the rate of interest paid on that monstrous burden – the national debt.

South America and South Africa were the two countries which chiefly participated in, and helped on, this period of inflation, which was as short as it was extraordinary. The history of the loans to the Argentine Republic, now that it has become history, is surprising indeed. A country which had a national debt of £10,000,000 in 1875, contrived to raise it to £70,000,000 in 1889. This, in addition to vast sums raised in Europe, on provincial credit, to carry out the innumerable railway concessions which were offered to, and accepted by, the eager investors in guaranteed" enterprises. All the money markets were competing with one another for a share of these good things. London, Paris, Brussels, Berlin, each was ready to outbid the other for the privilege of taking up ventures and floating loans which, at any other time, would have been regarded as very doubtful security, when the nature of the country, the character of the population, and the instability of its political institutions were carefully considered. They were not considered, however, and the investors of Great Britain, France, Belgium, and Germany had another opportunity of learning the value of Government guarantees south of the United States.

But at first and for some time all went well, especially with those to whom the loans were made. Buenos Ayres surpassed every other city in its luxury, extravagance, and wholesale squandering of wealth. There was literally no limit to the excesses of the wealthier classes. While money, luxuries, and material poured in on the one hand, crowds of immigrants from Italy and other countries flocked in to perpetuate the prosperity of the new Eldorado of the South. Railways, docks, tramways, water-works, gas-works, public buildings, mansions, all were being carried on at once in hot haste; and British and foreign contractors, engineers, and men of business did their best to increase the general eagerness to commence new undertakings.

But the facts are fresh in the minds of everyone. The character of the houses which took charge of the loans in London and on the Continent was so high that nobody could for the time doubt that all was well. That the Barings, the Murrietas and others were as careless and as greedy as houses of less name and fame, was not to be believed. It is a curious fact, as showing how little the real truth was generally appreciated, notwithstanding the warnings constantly given by the **Statist** newspaper, that the last railway loan successfully floated prior to the crash was subscribed for no less than eleven times over in London. And Uruguay gives only a repetition of the methods of the Argentine Republic on a smaller scale.

The real significance of this to English industry is not always appreciated fully. The money form of the loans disguises the fact that much of what is lent to the Argentine Republic, Uruguay, Brazil, Australia, etc., does not reach the borrowers in the shape of cash at all. The loan takes the form of works or manufactures of some sort, such as rails, bridges, pontoons,

134

articles of luxury, linen, cloth, etc., which means profit for the manufacturers and employment for the workers of England. But trade of this kind, fostered by loans from the country whose goods are ordered, must, in the very nature of the case, be precarious. As the loans fall off; owing to the security having been covered and no margin remaining, the trade falls off too, and cannot revive until, if the produce of the loans has been spent in development, a natural exchange of the products of the two countries is established. So long as the period of inflation lasted, however, business was good, the workers were fully employed, and could strike for higher wages with good hope of success for the time being, as the East End of London dockers did and many others. Prices and wages had once more risen to something like their old levels; orders could not be executed in consequence of the press of business – rails, for example, could not be had; the speculation had kept pace with the general prosperity; and yet all seemed so sound – for the Argentine and Uruguay are rich countries – that people thought the market in the spring and summer of 1890 might still hold out for another twelve or eighteen months, though that South America was over-borrowing was universally admitted. As a matter of fact, the collapse had even then begun; fears of a drain of gold to South America, as the premium on gold began to rise rapidly, scared shrewd observers; and the names of great financial firms were whispered about the city as being in serious difficulties.

Those who remember the collapse of Messrs. Over-end, Gurney & Co. twenty-six years ago say, that to men brought up in the City where this great firm had enjoyed unbounded influence and credit for two generations, it seemed inconceivable that the house should ever fall, even when it was generally known that its affairs were somewhat in disorder. When it did fall, a huge blank was occasioned which has never since been filled. All that men of business felt about Messrs. Overend, Gurney & Co. in 1856, and more than all, was felt in the city of London in 1889 about, the firm of Messrs. Baring

Bros. & Co. Lord Revelstoke, the head of the house, though an exceedingly arbitrary man, was looked upon as the first financier in the city. His ability, organising power, and foresight were extolled by all. Messrs. Baring had just floated Messrs. Guinness's brewery as a Limited Company with extraordinary success and profit to the firm, and had taken the *pas* of Messrs. Rothschild in the matter of financing the Manchester Ship Canal. Their mercantile business brought them in enormous profits yearly, and their name and credit were at this time the first in the world. There was a feeling of satisfaction throughout the country that a purely English house should stand so high at a time when German Jews held the leading place in nearly every great continental city.

And yet, at the very time when this was the general feeling, the Barings were allowing themselves to be cajoled into the acceptance, in conjunction with their syndicate, of some of the worst financial enterprises that any third-rate firm of financial adventurers ever tried to foist upon the public; and were straining their credit to an extent which even their capital and profits could not stand. The boasted ability of the greatest men in the city was again tried and found wanting, and Lord Revelstoke allowed himself to be completely bamboozled by an American adventurer, whose sole aim and object was to make commissions for himself. The story of Moses and the gross of green spectacles was told again in Bishopsgate Street to the tune of tens of millions of pounds sterling.

Suddenly a heavy fall in stocks, in which the Barings were known to be specially interested alike as owners and agents, and a pouring of Consols upon a depressed market, informed the public of what the private letter-books of the city, if they could be thrown open, would show was known to many firms long before. Then Russia was withdrawing gold from the great house at the same time; and it shortly became known that, unless exceptional steps were at once taken, another 1866 panic would be let loose upon the city. For the bank rate of discount was rapidly advancing; the great joint-stock banks were calling in their loans; gold was flowing out from the Bank of England, which itself was reported to hold £4,000,000 of the Barings' acceptances; and a fourth suspension of the Bank Act of 1844 was regarded as inevitable if matters were allowed to take their ordinary course. Then it was that the governor of the Bank of England, having assured himself of State support in case of need, adopted that plan of bolstering up rottenness, in the interest of the higher grade of financiers, of which the French had already given us more than one instance.

A guarantee fund was formed, in which the Bank of England took the lead, and every bank or firm of any note in the city joined, to ensure the meeting of the acceptances of Baring Brothers & Co. to the extent of £21,000,000; gold to the amount of £3,000,000 was borrowed by the Bank of England through the Rothschilds from the Bank of France, and more was obtained from Russia; the Barings' ordinary business was turned into a limited company, and – several other important firms went into a sort of limited liquidation. It was all thought to be a great stroke of genius at the time, and Mr. Lidderdale practically received the thanks of the Government, and was presented with the freedom of the city of London. The general opinion is not quite so favourable now, and it is quite possible that, when the circumstances come to be reviewed in the dry light of history, the Baring crisis of 1890, and the way in which it was met, will be cited as an example of the break-down of capitalism in the department of high finance.

That the whole crisis will be a permanent record of the imbecility of English investors there can already be no doubt whatever. For those who held Argentine bonds, to which they had subscribed on the faith of representations made by first-rate financial houses that had secured enormous profits out of the issues, actually allowed the representatives of these very houses to form a financial caucus, specially constituted to sacrifice the public interests of investors to their own private necessities; granting the Argentine Government an unasked-for delay in paying interest for three whole years, on condition that they, the magnates of the money market, should be relieved from their obligations in connection with the rotten scheme for the water-supply of the city of Buenos Ayres. Not a single bondholder (a shareholder was represented on this great committee, of which Lord Rothschild was the chairman, and the whole affair was arranged to the ruin of the investors so as to suit the pockets of those who sat with him round the table.

Since then the city of London has been in what may be called a state of permanent though suppressed panic. What is much more important, trade has steadily fallen off, and prices have, of course, as steadily shrunk. The exports to South America have gone down to such an extent that one great line of freight-carrying steamers, Messrs. Lamport & Holt's, has been practically without freight from this country for months past. The stagnation in the export trade, due to this South-American crisis; to the cessation for the time being of those Australian loans which likewise called for English produce; to the M'Kinley tariff in the United States, which has ruined the rough woollen trade of Bradford and the tin-plate trade of South Wales; to the increasing competition of foreign countries in the neutral markets; and to the disappointments in connection with South and Central Africa – this stagnation, though it may be brightened by temporary gleams of prosperity, threatens to be for a long time very prejudicial to the interests of the mass of the people.

During the short but sharp inflation of 1887 to 1890 the workers had been able to obtain advances of wages in many trades; and strikes for improved conditions of labour, of which the dockers' strike was the most famous, had been the rule rather than the exception. But mere strikes or Trade Union

138

combinations can no more change or influence the course of international commerce than a lecture on economics to a Zulu tribe. So long as the sole object of the production of wealth is the creation of surplus-value and profit, so long will the periods of bad trade follow periods of inflation, and so long will the workers who imagine that they have secured permanent advantages to-day find that, if dependent for the retention or those advantages merely on their own organisations, they have laid up for themselves uncertainty and disappointment for to-morrow.

Already the counter effects of the crisis of 1890 are making themselves felt in the money markets and industrial centres of France, Germany, Belgium, and other countries. The harmful conditions which permanently weigh upon the European situation – the vast loans raised for war purposes superadded to the already excessive indebtedness; the withdrawal of the flower of the population on the Continent at the most critical time of life from civil associations; the effect of American competition on agriculture, small and large; the undoubted fact that, with the increased power of machinery working at full speed, markets for commodities may be glutted in an incredibly short space of time – all these permanent causes for anxiety have been still further aggravated by the famine in Russia and the revolutionary movement in China, the consequences of which none can fully foresee. More than a year after the crisis of 1890 and the careful arrangements made to avoid a panic, the whole financial firmament of England is darkened by a cloud of distrust, and, in spite of a protracted period of caution and taking in of sail; there is all the doubt and uncertainty, or more than all the doubt and uncertainty, which would have followed had the crisis pursued the same course as those of 1857 and 1866.

Any attempt to fully analyse the effects of the crisis upon other countries would extend this little volume beyond the limits of its original plan. But it is apparent already that the extraordinary harvest in the United States, now having a population of 62,000,000, with 200,000 miles of railway, as well as the proportionately good harvest in Canada, must, in spite of all hostile tariffs, have a beneficial effect on the situation temporarily at least. It is even possible that the natural resources of the Argentine Republic, with its 90,000,000 sheep, 25,000,000 cattle, 7,000,000 acres of tilled land, and 7,000 miles of railway, may enable the comparatively sparse population to cope in part with its enormous load of debt if political quiet is maintained.

But the main facts of our modern industrial system remain unchanged by even the development of such vast natural wealth as that of North and South America. In the former great country the pressure of mortgages upon the farmers of the West, the vast railroad rings and industrial monopolies which have been built up, the impossibility so far of obtaining any control for or by the people of the huge machine of capitalism even under democratic and republican forms, leave the mass of the producers as much at the mercy of the money-lords as they are in Europe, and the crises of the United States have been in some respects worse than those of the old world. In the Argentina, difficulties have but just begun; but there also, what is perhaps the finest undeveloped country in the world, has not protected some of the most industrious, sober, and thrifty immigrants that ever went out to seek their fortune from undergoing starvation and misery, where they looked for well-being and happiness in return for hard work.

X. Remedies

Having thus come to an end of this brief and necessarily very incomplete sketch of the great industrial crises of the nineteenth century covering the entire period, from the time when steam had become the chief engine in modern production and transportation to the date when electricity was manifestly being made ready to take in turn the superior place, certain main features strike us most forcibly.

Industrial crises and the consequent over-population which they create are quite independent –

1. Of population whether rapidly increasing or stationary, as may be seen from the instances of Great Britain and France.

2. Of forms of Government, whether they be despotic, constitutional-monarchic, or republican.

3. Of extent of territory and unoccupied land, as witness the United States, Australia, and the Argentine Republic.

4. Of restricted or inflated currency; of the gold or silver standard.

5. Of any special system of banking; the soundest methods doing no more than limit the range of the calamity: the least sound doing no more than extend it.

6. Of free-trade or protection. Free-trade affords no protection: protection guarantees no free-trade.

Yet we have in these crises manifestly social cataclysms which are caused by the action of man in society, and which man in society can master when he comprehends what is going on around him.

In order to do away with these recurrent crises and

141

collapses of trade, we have to harmonise the two sides of wealth-creation, and to lead the way to the period when production having already become, as it, has become, purely social, appropriation and exchange shall become purely social too.

In order to bring this about, the organised power of the State, of the Municipal Council, of the District Assembly, each acting in concert and co-operation with the other, must step in to reduce to order the existing anarchy, which produces such baneful effects, and to establish an equilibrium between production, consumption, and general distribution for the benefit of all. Whatever name we may call this by, it involves organised co-operation in which every adult member of the community will take an intelligent and active part.

But we have not arrived at the time when the majority of the people can regard land, machinery, raw material, and the useful products which are the result of the application of labour to this land, machinery, and raw material, except from the point of view of private property and profit to the individual.

That is quite true, and that is why, if we wish to put a stop to the present anarchy and solve the present economical, and therefore social and class, antagonism without bloodshed and bitter war, it is necessary to show that the course of human development is at the present time towards this period of social harmony, instead of sticking fast in the existing muddle as some contend. To show, that is, that mankind in all civilised countries is at this very moment proceeding, unconsciously and with much trouble and suffering, to bring about that which, if the community were acting consciously, could be done much more rapidly and without any suffering at all.

Now we have seen how capitalists themselves are all the time turning their individual businesses, whether distributive or productive, into limited companies. But this is distinctly a step towards socialisation, inasmuch that it at once becomes

142

apparent that a body of shareholders, who know nothing whatever about the business of which they are by a legal convention the owners, and who employ a manager to conduct the concern for them, are by no means more capable of carrying it on than are those whom they employ to do the work; seeing that the workers might with equal fitness retain, if necessary, the same manager as has been appointed by the shareholders.

The companies, however, when formed, are now as anxious to restrict competition as formerly they were to intensify it. They have discovered, of course entirely in their own interests, that an unceasing competition to produce cheaper and cheaper means that when the smaller firms are crushed out the bigger firms must ruin one another too. None wishes to risk all on the chance of surviving the whole of his competitors. Hence the tendency, continually growing stronger in spite of failures, for combination to replace competition in the sphere of production, as it leas already done to a great extent in the field of transport and distribution.

This combination, if carried sufficiently far, may, and even now in part does, limit "over-production" and maintain prices in certain trades, but it cannot harmonise the interests of the wage-earners with the interests of the employers; because it must always be to the advantage of employers, whether individuals or companies, to make use of improved machinery in order to maintain the agreed rate of output with a less expenditure of labour. This would necessarily entail a discharge of some of those persons who were previously employed, and one of the worst features of crisis would equally appear as before in a number of people thrown out of work by the very improvement of the means of creating wealth. Moreover, the surplus population thus engendered would be in competition with their fellows in employment and the rate of wages must eventually be reduced. Combination between employers will probably follow to keep up prices. By degrees, in ordinary circumstances, the combination might be broken down as we have seen it was in the instances of copper and salt. But the tendency of large companies to restrict that free competition, which not long ago was the watchword of the capitalist class, is clearly manifested in the United States and in Great Britain, and in some cases, such as the Standard Oil Company of America and the screw trade of Birmingham, a practical monopoly has been successfully maintained for many years.

But if it is to the interest of the capitalist class to change their tactics, whereby they have gained supremacy, in order to keep up a rate of profits threatened by the very keenness of their own competition; if also the large capitals are beating the small, and companies and co-operative stores are absorbing or crushing individual producers and distributors as we see they are; it cannot be but to the advantage of the whole community that some steps should be taken to control or to handle the increasing powers which are thus growing up under the protection of the law.

For on the other side, as likewise the history of this century shows us, the workers themselves are beginning to understand better than ever the essential truths of that antagonism between social production and individual or company appropriation of which we have spoken. They, too, are more anxious than ever they were to lessen the competition which reduces their wages, and to remove the causes of those ups and downs of trade which occasion their excessive work at overtime in one year, only to be followed by worklessness and low wages in the next. Nor are their combinations any longer confined to the skilled trades or to one country. In the same way that capitalists gather together in international banks, international promoting agencies, and international industrial enterprises, regardless of that patriotism which is frequently appealed to; in like manner the workers also are banding themselves together as a class internationally against the controllers of the system of production which, being based upon profit only, is worked entirely contrary to their interest. They thus give expression in the shape of long strikes, and vigorous protests wherever they can get a hearing, to that economic antagonism which they feel themselves to be the victims of. Machines are now no longer broken nor are factories burnt down. The workers' object now is to preserve, in order to take possession of and control, the growing forces of production which are being used against them.

It is this class antagonism, developed on a larger scale than ever before in every civilised country, which has rendered the social question the one important question of the time; which gave rise to the Berlin Labour Conference, and which has set on foot the Royal Commission on Labour. To say that it ought not to exist is intelligible: to state that it does not exist is absurd.

That the necessity for a solution is being recognised in Great Britain cannot be disputed. The capitalists themselves are shaken in their confidence of being able to handle their own machinery. The long slow drag prior to the last period of inflation and then the Baring crash opened the eyes of many of the manufacturers, while the existing uncertainty is influencing many more. The literary class and professional men, who are not directly interested in the manipulation of profits, are already even better prepared to accept the Social-Democratic or Collectivist solution which is inevitable than are the workers themselves.

Now the influence of the State, as the organised force of the community, has all the while been extending, and, so strong is the pressure of the current of events upon politicians and the House of Commons, that almost every measure proposed by either political party is avowedly or unavowedly founded upon Collectivist as opposed to Individualist theories.

The problem is to reduce the existing anarchy to order,

in face of the development of international crises and the growing international solidarity of the capitalist class. This is manifestly no easy matter to solve even in Great Britain, the country which, owing to its economical development, its commercial and financial position, its preponderance of great cities, and its geographical situation, must inevitably take the lead in any important social transformation. For England, more than any other nation, is dependent upon foreign countries so largely, and in some cases so exclusively, for her supplies of food and the raw materials of her manufactures, that nothing can be done without touching exterior interests at some point.

Nevertheless, any attempt at regulation and reorganisation must begin in one nation first, and England, which took the lead in the development of the capitalist system, seems destined to take the lead also in its transformation. Thus the needs of the home market within certain limits could easily be ascertained, and would be easily ascertained now if our statistical departments were not so miserably behind-hand. The State, for example, in addition to being the greatest employer of labour in the country by far, is also directly and indirectly the greatest consumer.

Leaving aside the temporary advantage which would result by the absorption of unemployed labour from the enactment by law of an Eight Hours' Day and the suppression of overtime for all State workers, together with the consequently increased demand for goods, it is obvious that an average of the requirements of all employees might easily be arrived at, in so far as the necessaries of life are concerned, even as matters stand to-day. The enactment of a minimum wage of say 30s. or 35s. a week would only mean that the standard of life in the lower grades of labour would be raised, and, therefore, the demand for such necessaries would again increase.

But if we add to the numbers who are directly employed

146

by the State the persons who are indirectly employed, such as those who supply clothes, boots, and food to the Government servants, including, of course, the army, navy, and militia; to these add the colliers who supply coal, the ironworkers who supply iron, and others who in turn supply them; if again we consider the men and women employed by our various municipalities and other local authorities, and the workers who supply them; and if we further add to the numbers of the State and municipal functionaries and servants the tens of thousands of men who are engaged on railways and other monopolies – if we calculate all these producers and distributors as a portion of the recognised or unrecognised public service, we arrive at very large figures indeed. So far as they are concerned there need be no ups and downs of trade; for the object here at least must be – assuming for the moment the elimination of the middleman and the capitalist, in the same way as he is eliminated in a Government establishment – to bring consumers and producers together without profit, to the common gain. Instead of this even State contracts have, until lately, been conducted on the sweating system, and all labour employed by the State has been beaten down to the lowest competitive wage. Worse still, in the Government arsenals and factories excessive overtime is worked at some periods, though outside thousands are unemployed; and at other periods men are discharged for lack of work to give them.

But, manifestly, if the Government under the control of the profit-making classes is compelled to keep up State arsenals and dockyards, State post-office and parcel post, State banks and factories; and at the same time municipalities are taking control of their gasworks, and water-works, and tramways, and road-making, and in some degree of public building; there can be no insuperable difficulty in extending the operations of the State and municipalities to the various productive enterprises which supply these State and municipal bodies with what they need.

Unfortunately, all our leading statesmen and officials, all our principal economists and publicists, have been brought up in a school which disenables them from looking at the production and distribution of wealth as a public, collective business. Their anxiety for the welfare of the individual is so great that they crush individuality by competition: they so love order that they foster industrial anarchy: they so dread the State that they favour the growth of practically irresponsible and uncontrolled monopolies such as we see all around us.

But workers are increasingly anxious to use the collective power for the advantage of the community, and to master through the State and municipal organisations the great productive and distributive agencies alike of the Government and of private companies, so as to attain that end. When once we admit that the increased power to produce wealth should be thus used for the benefit of the many and not for the profit of the few, no long time will elapse thereafter before steps are taken, by collective organisation of industry and exchange, to prevent the periodical dislocation of trade by great crises, which are as wasteful as they are in a sense absurd.

There is no possibility of reducing the existing anarchy in production and distribution to order by anything short of this collective ownership of the great means and instruments of production and distribution. This inevitably involves the overthrow of private property or company ownership of those great means and instruments of creating and distributing wealth. And this again carries with it the disappearance of the class State, and the establishment of an organised communism in which private ownership will be confined within the narrowest possible limits.

Those who talk of "Municipal Socialism" as if it were possible to segregate mankind into petty little units with no power to regulate the general production, first nationally and then internationally, overlook the most striking features of the

148

economic development which is going on around them. In like manner, the proposal to ameliorate existing conditions by taxation of rent, disregards the truth that modern rents presuppose the existence of competition and take for granted that capitalist supremacy, which such taxation, even were it possible to carry it into effect, would leave untouched.

Mere palliatives, such as those which have been advocated for years by the Social-Democratic Federation, and are now being adopted in some shape by both the existing capitalist political factions, are, after all, but palliatives; although the men who have been most active in championing them, have carried on this "practical" propaganda with the direct object of preparing the way to a complete and, if possible, peaceful transformation. But wage-slaves under better conditions remain wage-slaves still; and the causes of the economic and class antagonism remain untouched by any half-measures. No improvements of the capitalist system of production can change or seriously modify the bitter struggle which must go on so long as that system endures in any shape.

The time is coming when the expropriators will be themselves expropriated, and it is for the rising generation of Englishmen to decide whether in this country the substitution of organised co-operation for anarchical competition shall be brought about consciously and peacefully, or unconsciously and forcibly. The next commercial crisis, which all careful observers can easily detect is approaching, will, by reason of the tremendous scale on which production is now carried on in every civilised country, be worse than any yet experienced. The issue of one pound notes in such circumstances is, indeed, to administer a pill to an earthquake. Such an issue can no more prevent a commercial crisis in the nineties than a similar issue did in the twenties; and Mr. Goschen's proposal will probably be referred to in time to come as a remarkable instance of the incapacity of our ablest financiers to reason outside of the limited and vicious circle of capitalist finance.

Nine recognised commercial crises in this nineteenth century, all deeply affecting the welfare of Great Britain and other civilised countries, and each in succession having a more enduring influence for evil than its forerunner, must surely prove to every one who is not blinded by his own supposed interests that capitalism has outlived its usefulness, and must be replaced by another and higher form of industrial and social organisation. After such terrible warnings, to refuse to examine into facts, and to proceed farther on the happy-go-lucky principle of awaiting "pressure from without," is only to court that disaster which pessimists declare is inevitable, do what we may.

THE END

www.ingramcontent.com/pod-product-compliance
Lightning Source LLC
Chambersburg PA
CBHW070021300526
45794CB00001B/385